¡Viva el español!

Workbook
Annotated
Teacher's Edition

¡Adelante!

John De Mado
Linda Tibensky

Jane Jacobsen-Brown
Christine Wolinski Szeszol
Donna Alfredo Wardanian

Marcela Gerber, Series Consultant

Wright Group

The **McGraw·Hill** Companies

www.WrightGroup.com

 **Wright Group**

Copyright ©2005 Wright Group/McGraw-Hill

All rights reserved. Except as permitted under the United States Copyright Act, no part of this publication may be reproduced or distributed in any form or by any means, or stored in a database or retrieval system, without the prior written permission from the publisher, unless otherwise indicated.

Printed in the United States of America.

Send all inquiries to:
Wright Group/McGraw-Hill
P.O. Box 812960
Chicago, Illinois 60681

ISBN: 0-07-602942-5

2 3 4 5 6 7 8 9 MAZ 10 09 08 07 06 05 04

Contenido

Nombre _Jordan_

A. You are visiting the Chiflado family, the world's best ventriloquists! Guess who is doing the talking. Beside each statement, write the name of the person or animal who probably said it, based on what you see in the picture.

M _____Hugo_____ Estoy en el jardín. ¡Me gustan las cerezas!

1. _____Mamá_____ El tigre y yo estamos en el dormitorio.

2. _____José_____ ¡Por fin! La mariposa está muy cerca.

3. _____Papá_____ ¿Dónde está el perro? ¡Ay! ¡Tengo miedo!

4. _____Gatitos_____ Estamos en la cocina. ¿Dónde está la leche?

5. _____Óscar_____ ¡Qué bonito está el día! Mi tortuga y yo estamos fuera de la casa.

6. _____Luisa_____ ¡Pobrecito! Mi pez y yo estamos en el patio. El pez tiene mucha hambre.

Extension: Follow up the exercise by asking questions about the picture (for example, **¿Quiénes están dentro de la casa?**).

Nombre _____

B. Look at this living room and kitchen. Can you tell where everything is? Use *delante de, detrás de, cerca de y lejos de.*

La sala de estar

M (el retrato/el estéreo) _____ **El retrato está detrás del estéreo.** _____

1. (el sofá/el televisor) _____ El sofá está delante del televisor. _____

2. (el sillón/la estantería) _____ El sillón está delante de la estantería. _____

3. (el televisor/el estéreo) _____ El televisor está cerca del estéreo. _____

4. (el estante/el sofá) _____ El estante está detrás del sofá. _____

La cocina

M (el refrigerador/la estufa) _____ El refrigerador está cerca de la estufa. _____

1. (la mesa/el fregadero) _____ La mesa está delante del fregadero. _____

2. (la silla/la mesa) _____ La silla está detrás de la mesa. _____

3. (el retrato/el teléfono) _____ El retrato está lejos del teléfono. _____

Nombre _____

C. What does your dream house look like, inside and out? Describe it.

Ⓜ Tiene el techo rosado. Hay 10 habitaciones. _____

_____ Answers will vary. _____

_____

_____

D. The students in the nurse's office are all complaining about their aches and pains. What do they say? Write a sentence saying what hurts each person.

Ⓜ ADÁN: ¡Ay, me duelen los pies! _____

1. MATEO: ¡Ay, me duele el codo! _____

2. LUPE: ¡Ay, me duelen las manos! _____

3. PEDRO: ¡Ay, me duelen los dedos! _____

4. HUGO: ¡Ay, me duele el brazo! _____

Nombre _____

E. Your friend Manuel has come with you to shop for new clothes. He has strong opinions about clothes, and doesn't hesitate to let you know what he thinks! Write your question and Manuel's answer, based on the words given.

M el suéter / pequeño   Manuel, ¿cómo me queda el suéter? _____

¡Mal! Ese suéter te queda pequeño. _____

1. el abrigo /pequeño   Manuel, ¿cómo me queda el abrigo? _____

¡Mal! El abrigo te queda pequeño. _____

2. la camiseta / corta   Manuel, ¿cómo me queda la camiseta? _____

¡Mal! La camiseta te queda corta. _____

3. los pantalones / largos   Manuel, ¿cómo me quedan los pantalones? _____

¡Mal! Los pantalones te quedan largos. _____

F. Look at the picture on page 5 and write sentences using the adjectives below and *más, menos, el más* or *la más* and *la menos* or *el menos.* Change the form of the words if you need it.

✓bajo   guapo   tímido   atlético   simpático   antipático

M El señor Gómez es el más bajo. _____

1. Answers will vary. _____

2. _____

3. _____

4. _____

5. _____

Nombre _____

G. Test your powers of observation. Write the name of each person under each picture. (Careful! There are more people than sentences!)

M El señor Gómez no tiene mucho pelo. Lleva unos pantalones y una camisa.

1. Amalia tiene el pelo corto y rizado. Lleva una camisa y unos pantalones.

2. Javier tiene el pelo negro y corto. Lleva una camiseta y unos pantalones cortos.

3. Elena es guapa. Lleva unos pantalones y una blusa.

4. Diana tiene el pelo rubio y largo. Lleva una camiseta y unos pantalones.

Es Amalia.   Es Elena.   Es Javier.   **Es el señor** _____   Es Diana.

Gómez

Enrichment: Students may enjoy finding pictures in old magazines to create their own guessing game of matching descriptions to people.

Nombre _____

H. Esperanza wrote two paragraphs about a typical school morning. Help her finish the paragraphs.

You may wish to use activity H for dictation practice.

Mis amigas y yo _____vivimos_____ muy cerca de la escuela. En la mañana
(vivir)

nosotras _____caminamos_____ a la escuela. Los conserjes _____abren_____ las
(caminar)   (abrir)

puertas a las ocho en punto.

A las ocho y media mis amigas _____tienen_____ la clase de arte. Yo
(tener)

_____tengo_____ la clase de ciencias. Yo _____acabo_____ de comenzar una
(tener)   (acabar)

clase nueva. A veces _____voy_____ a la clase a las ocho y cuarto porque
(ir)

_____quiero_____ ayuda con las lecciones. A mí _____me gustan_____ las
(querer)   (gustar)

ciencias, pero no _____comprendo_____ todas las lecciones. Los maestros siempre
(comprender)

_____ayudan_____ a los alumnos con sus problemas. La clase
(ayudar)

_____acaba_____ de comenzar. ¡Luego _____escribo_____ más!
acabar   escribir

Extension: The paragraphs may serve as a model for students' original compositions.

Nombre _____

I. Rebeca has invited Javier and Alicia for breakfast. They are now preparing everything. Look at the picture and complete the dialogue with *traer, poner,* or *gustar* in the correct form.

M REBECA: ¡Hola Alicia! ¿Qué _____**traes**_____?

ALICIA: _____**Traigo**_____ cerezas y fresas.

JAVIER: ¡Qué bien! A mí _____**me gustan**_____ mucho las cerezas.

REBECA: ¿_____**Traes**_____ también chocolate y leche?

ALICIA: Sí. A mí no _____**me gusta**_____ la leche, ¿a ustedes

_____**les gusta**_____, verdad?

JAVIER: A nosotros _____**nos gusta**_____ mucho.

REBECA: También tenemos pan, mermelada y mantequilla.

REBECA: _____**Pongo**_____ la mesa, aquí tengo el mantel y las servilletas.

JAVIER: Yo _____**pongo**_____ las tazas y los platos.

¿_____**Pones**_____ las cucharas y los cuchillos, Alicia?

ALICIA: Sí, claro.

JAVIER: ¡Qué rico todo!

Extension: Have students check their answers by forming groups of three and reading the dialogue out loud.

Nombre _____

J. You have to do chores before *(antes de)* dinner, and you have to study after *(después de)* dinner. You want to know if other students have the same schedule. Use the words in parentheses to write your friends' answers.

You may wish to give examples of **antes de** and **después de** before assigning this activity. Write a time on the chalkboard and talk about your activities before that time and after that time.

M Juan y Andrés, ¿qué tienen que hacer antes de la cena?
(estudiar y poner la mesa)

Tenemos que estudiar y poner la mesa.

1. Tonia, ¿qué tienes que hacer después de la cena?
(lavar y secar los platos)

Tengo que lavar y secar los platos.

2. Darío y Antonio, ¿qué tienen que hacer antes de la cena?
(regar las plantas y sacar la basura)

Tenemos que regar las plantas y sacar la basura.

3. Susana, ¿qué tienen que hacer tus hermanos después de la cena?
(pasar la aspiradora y escribir cartas)

Tienen que pasar la aspiradora y escribir cartas.

4. Mateo, ¿qué tienes que hacer antes de la cena?
(barrer el piso y quitar el polvo)

Tengo que barrer el piso y quitar el polvo.

5. Beatriz, ¿qué tienen que hacer tus hermanas después de la cena?
(¡nada!)

¡No tienen que hacer nada!

Extension: Continue by asking students what they have to do before dinner and after dinner.

Nombre _____

K. Graciela wants to become friends with you. What do you have in common? Answer her questions in your own words.

M Mi familia y yo pensamos ir al teatro el sábado. ¿Adónde piensan ir tu familia y tú?

Pensamos ir al mercado el sábado. _____

1. Mis clases comienzan a las nueve. ¿A qué hora comienzan tus clases?

Students' answers will vary. _____

2. Yo puedo patinar bien. ¿Puedes tú patinar?

_____

3. Mi familia quiere ir a México. ¿Adónde quieren ir ustedes?

_____

4. Almuerzo a las once y media. ¿A qué hora almuerzan tus amigos y tú?

_____

L. The Garcías invited Graciela to dinner. Complete the sentences with the correct form of the verbs to tell what Graciela does to get ready to go.

Primero, ___**se quita**___ la ropa sucia. Luego, ___**se baña**___ y
       (quitarse)   (bañarse)

___**se seca**___. Por último, ___**se peina**___ y ___**se pone**___
   (secarse)   (peinarse)   (ponerse)

ropa limpia. Ahora ___**se va**___ de la casa. Los García y ella
                      (irse)

___**van**___ a cenar.
   (ir)

You may wish to use activity L for dictation practice, changing from first person singular to first person plural forms (for example, **nos quitamos**).

Nombre _____

M. You're talking to a new student about the different people who work in your school and where they work. First unscramble the letters. Then write one sentence about each person's job, and a second sentence telling where they work.

M La señora López (dcetairro)

La señora López es la directora. Trabaja en la oficina.

_____

1. el señor Quesada (meorrefne)

   El señor Quesada es el enfermero. Trabaja en la enfermería.

   _____

2. el señor Cervantes (icorenoc)

   El señor Cervantes es el cocinero. Trabaja en el comedor.

   _____

3. la señorita Fuentes (oatiriabcelbi)

   La señorita Fuentes es la bibliotecaria. Trabaja en la biblioteca.

   _____

4. el señor Meléndez (eesstntai aisiainvtortmd)

   El señor Meléndez es el asistente administrativo. Trabaja en la oficina.

5. el señor Ramírez (rjcesone)

   El señor Ramírez es el conserje. Answers will vary about where he works.

¿Cómo se dice?

Nombre _____

Textbook pages 24–27

A. These children are talking about their favorite sports. Can you name them?

M
Nos gusta mucho _____**el fútbol**_____.

1.
Me gusta _____*el béisbol*_____.

2.
Nos gusta _____*el baloncesto*_____.

3.
Me gusta _____*el tenis*_____.

4.
Nos gusta _____*el fútbol americano*_____.

5.
Me gusta _____*el volibol*_____.

Extension: Have students write their own sentences about which of these sports they like or don't like.

¿Cómo se dice?

Textbook pages 28–32

Nombre _____

A. Look at this list of hobbies. Which of these can be practiced indoors and which can be practiced outdoors? Write them in the correct column. Then write a check mark next to your favorite activities.

Note that while some activities, such as playing an instrument or playing chess can be practiced outdoors, they are mostly practiced indoors. However, taking photographs can be in both columns. Accept reasonable answers.

jugar al ajedrez

sacar fotos

jugar a las damas

jugar al dominó

jugar a los juegos electrónicos

coleccionar estampillas

montar a caballo

tocar un instrumento

cultivar plantas

ir de pesca

ir en bicicleta

Fuera

ir de pesca _____

ir en bicicleta _____

montar a caballo _____

sacar fotos _____

cultivar plantas _____

_____

_____

Dentro

jugar al ajedrez _____

tocar un instrumento _____

jugar a las damas _____

jugar al dominó _____

jugar a los juegos electrónicos _____

coleccionar estampillas _____

sacar fotos _____

Extension: Have students talk in pairs about their hobbies, using **"Me gusta..."** or **"Mis pasatiempos favoritos son..."**

¿Cómo se dice?

Textbook pages 33–37

Nombre _____

A. Who plays what? Join the parts of the sentences to find out and write the sentences.

Note that subjects **Tus amigos y tu** and **Sofia y Ruben** can be matched with two different options.

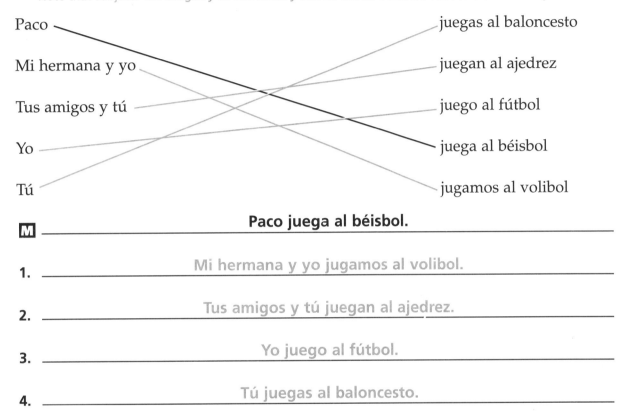

Paco — juegas al baloncesto

Mi hermana y yo — juegan al ajedrez

Tus amigos y tú — juego al fútbol

Yo — juega al béisbol

Tú — jugamos al volibol

M _____ **Paco juega al béisbol.** _____

1. _____ Mi hermana y yo jugamos al volibol. _____

2. _____ Tus amigos y tú juegan al ajedrez. _____

3. _____ Yo juego al fútbol. _____

4. _____ Tú juegas al baloncesto. _____

Now, make up new sentences joining the subjects with a different activity and changing the verb as needed.

M _____ **Paco juega al fútbol.** _____

1. _____ Answers will vary. _____

2. _____

3. _____

4. _____

Nombre _____

B. Do you and your friends have hobbies? Do you play sports? Write questions for these answers.

M **¿Cuándo juegas al fútbol?** _____

Juego al fútbol en el verano.

1. ¿Cuándo juegan ustedes al baloncesto? _____

Jugamos al baloncesto en el invierno.

2. ¿David juega al fútbol americano los fines de semana? _____

Sí, David juega al fútbol americano los fines de semana.

3. ¿Cuándo juego al ajedrez? _____

Juegas al ajedrez en el invierno.

4. ¿Jugamos a las damas en verano? _____

No, ustedes no juegan a las damas en el verano.

5. ¿Juegas al béisbol en verano? _____

Sí, juego al béisbol en el verano.

6. ¿Cuándo juegan al volibol? _____

Juegan al volibol en verano.   **Extension:** Have students think of other activities related to seasons or times of the day. You may start them off with questions (for example, **¿Cuando van de pesca? ¿Cuándo cultivan plantas?**).

C. What sports or games do you play well? What sports or games do you not play well? Write three sentences.

M Juego muy bien al ajedrez.

Juego muy mal al fútbol.

1. Answers will vary. _____

2. _____

3. _____

Students may work in pairs to create mini-conversations:
S1: No juego bien al tenis.
S2: Yo juego muy mal al tenis también. Tú juegas bien al volibol.

¿Cómo se dice?

Nombre _____

Textbook pages 38–41

A. Antonia and Timoteo are trying to improve themselves. They are discussing their strengths and weaknesses. Complete their conversation by writing the correct form of *ser* in each blank.

ANTONIA: Tú _____**eres**_____ un buen jugador, ¿verdad?

TIMOTEO: Sí, a veces ___**soy**___ un buen jugador. Tú también ___**eres**___
una buena jugadora.

ANTONIA: Gracias, Timoteo. Nosotros ___**somos**___ simpáticos, ¿verdad?

TIMOTEO: Sí. Pero a veces yo ___**soy**___ un poco impaciente. Mi papá y mi
hermano ___**son**___ impacientes también.

ANTONIA: A veces yo ___**soy**___ tímida. Mi amiga Lucinda ___**es**___
tímida también.

TIMOTEO: Tú y yo ___**somos**___ muy inteligentes, ¿verdad?

ANTONIA: ¡Claro que sí! Pero no ___**somos**___ muy modestos.

Extension: You may wish to use this exercise for dictation practice.

Nombre _____

B. Alberto is trying to write about the people in his school. Help him out by writing a complete sentence on each line using the words given.

Help students note the omission of definite and indefinite articles in the sentences.

M El Sr. Campos / conserje _____ **El Sr. Campos es conserje.** _____

M Elena y yo / alumno _____ **Elena y yo somos alumnos.** _____

1. La Sra. Oviedo / enfermera _____ La Sra. Oviedo es enfermera. _____

2. Juan y Luis / jugador _____ Juan y Luis son jugadores. _____

3. Estela / jugadora _____ Estela es jugadora (también). _____

4. El Sr. Torres y la Srta. Cano / maestro _____ El Sr. Torres y la Srta. Cano son maestros.

_____

5. Carla, Raúl y yo / alumno _____ Carla, Raúl y yo somos alumnos. _____

C. What traits do you share with a friend or with a member of your family? Are you tall? Are you generous? Are you impatient? Write five sentences.

M Mi amiga y yo somos inteligentes.

M Mi hermano y yo somos altos y delgados.

1. Sentences will vary. _____

2. _____

3. _____

4. _____

5. _____

¡A leer!

Nombre _____

Read the following paragraph *(el párrafo)* and answer the questions.

Tiempo libre

Usamos nuestro tiempo libre de maneras diferentes. A algunas personas les gusta jugar al ajedrez, a otras les gusta tocar el piano, la guitarra, el violín o la trompeta; algunas siempre van de vacaciones y otras, nunca. Hay personas que cultivan plantas y personas que juegan a los juegos electrónicos muchas horas, con la computadora.

A algunos nos gusta jugar o ver deportes como el fútbol o el béisbol. Jugar al fútbol es más divertido que mirar a los jugadores, pero los jugadores necesitan también oír "¡Hurras!" y "¡Vivas!" para poder jugar bien. Los músicos del equipo tocan los tambores y las trompetas para animar al equipo.

Escribe cosas del párrafo que las personas juegan y cosas que las personas tocan.

jugar	tocar
al ajedrez	el piano
a los juegos electrónicos	la guitarra
al fútbol	el violín
al béisbol	la trompeta
	los tambores

Now choose your five favorite activities from the chart above and write sentences with each of them.

_____

_____

_____

_____

_____

Nombre _____

Conexión con las matemáticas

Look at all these people and teams. Under each team, write how many people there are and what they play.

M **Nueve jugadores juegan al béisbol.**

_____

Once jugadores juegan al fútbol americano.

_____

Cinco jugadoras juegan al baloncesto.

_____

Dos jugadores juegan al tenis.

_____

Ocho jugadoras juegan al fútbol.

_____

What's the total amount of players on this page? What's the average number of people for all of the teams? Write your calculations below.

Expresa tus ideas

Nombre _____

The members of the Explorers' Club would rather be exploring or hiking or doing just about anything other than sitting in math class. What are they doing in their daydreams? Write at least eight sentences about what you see them doing in the picture.

Students' sentences will vary. Possible sentences include: El maestro de

matemáticas es impaciente. Nadie estudia las matemáticas. Paco juega al béisbol.

Es un jugador muy bueno. A Rita le gusta la música. Ella toca muchos

instrumentos. Luis va de pesca. Tiene un pez muy grande. Pepe y José juegan al

fútbol americano. Ellos juegan muy bien. Ana juega al ajedrez con su abuelo.

Berta monta a caballo. También saca fotos.

_____

_____

_____

☺ ¡A DIVERTIRSE! ☺   Nombre _____

¡Nombra la actividad!

Imagine that you are on the television game show "¡Nombra la actividad!" You have five minutes to look at pictures and name the activities that go with them.

 ir de pesca _____

_____

 el dominó _____

_____

 el volibol _____

_____

 el béisbol _____

_____

 montar a caballo _____

_____

 leer libros _____

_____

 cultivar plantas _____

_____

 tocar un instrumento _____

_____

 ir en bicicleta _____

_____

Your time is up! Now for the bonus point!

 sacar fotos _____

_____

el fútbol _____

_____

Extension: You may wish to time students and ring a bell when five minutes have passed. Students who name the most activities correctly may receive a prize (such as no homework for the evening).

¿Cómo se dice?

Nombre _____

Textbook pages 46–49

○ **A.** Can you recognize the places and people in this picture? Write the letters of the places and people you can see next to their names.

M el bombero _____h_____

1. el hospital _____a_____   6. la estación de bomberos _____b_____

2. el médico _____d_____   7. la médica _____f_____

3. la policía _____j_____   8. el policía _____k_____

4. el paciente _____e_____   9. la paciente _____g_____

5. la estación de policía _____c_____   10. la bombera _____i_____

¿Cómo se dice?

Textbook pages 50–53

Nombre _____

A. Are you a good observer? Look at these people and say what they do and where they work.

M Es una vendedora. Trabaja en la tienda por departamentos.

_____

1.  Es un obrero. Trabaja en una fábrica.

_____

2.  Es un empleado. Trabaja en una compañía.

_____

3.  Es la dueña. Trabaja en una compañía.

_____

4.  Es un bombero. Trabaja en una estación de bomberos.

_____

5.  Es una médica. Trabaja en un hospital.

_____

6.  Es un policía. Trabaja en una estación de policía.

_____

¿Cómo se dice?

Nombre _____

Textbook pages 54–57

○ **A.** You are having a party at your house. You want to know if the guests
know one another. Complete each conversation by writing the correct
form of *conocer.*

M

P: Estela, ¿_____**conoces**_____ a Inés?

R: Sí, _____**conozco**_____ a Inés.

1.

P: Sergio, ¿_____conoces_____ a Chela y a Mari?

R: No, no _____conozco_____ a Chela y a Mari.

2.

P: Ana y Tere, _____conocen_____ a Eduardo?

R: Sí, _____conocemos_____ a Eduardo.

3.

P: Sra. Vélez, ¿_____conoce_____ al Sr. Maldonado?

R: Sí, _____conozco_____ muy bien al Sr. Maldonado.

4.

P: Pepe y Leo, ¿_____conocen_____ a la Srta. Burgos?

R: No, no _____conocemos_____ a la Srta. Burgos.

Nombre _____

B. Whom do you and your friends know in your community? Read each question, then answer according to whom you know and don't know.

M ¿Tus amigos y tú conocen una vendedora?

Sí, conocemos una vendedora. Se llama Elena Rojas.

1. ¿Conoces un policía?

Answers will vary. _____

2. ¿Tus amigos y tú conocen un obrero?

_____

3. ¿Tus amigos y tú conocen un jugador de fútbol americano?

_____

4. ¿Conoces al dueño de una compañía?

_____

5. ¿Conoces a un bombero?

_____

6. ¿Tus amigos y tú conocen una enfermera?

_____

¿Cómo se dice?

Textbook pages 58–61

Nombre _____

○ **A.** You have been watching too many spy movies. You're sneaking around to observe people and take notes on their activities! Complete each sentence with the correct form of the verb.

M Son las ocho. Tomás está ___**sacando**___ la basura.
(sacar)

1. Son las nueve y media. Judit está ___comiendo___ una manzana.
(comer)

2. Son las diez. El policía está ___ayudando___ a un hombre.
(ayudar)

3. Son las diez y cuarto. Mamá está ___abriendo___ la puerta.
(abrir)

4. Son las once. Un obrero está ___caminando___ a la fábrica.
(caminar)

5. Son las doce. Juan y yo estamos ___almorzando___.
(almorzar)

6. Son las dos. Papá está ___trabajando___ en el jardín.
(trabajar)

7. Son las tres. Dos niños están ___corriendo___ cerca de mi casa.
(correr)

8. Son las tres y media. Me duele la mano porque estoy ___escribiendo___ mucho.
(escribir)

Nombre _____

B. You are asking your sister who in the neighborhood is singing like an injured moose! How does she answer you?

¿Canta Carlos?

No. Está pintando.

_____

5.

¿Cantan Ana y Pablo?

No. Están planchando.

_____

1.

¿Canta Diana?

No. Está bailando.

_____

6.

¿Cantan Iris y Luis?

No. Están nadando.

_____

2.

¿Canta Manuel?

No. Está escribiendo.

_____

7.

¿Canta Pepe?

No. Está poniendo

la mesa.

_____

3.

¿Canta Jorge?

No. Está comiendo.

_____

8.

¿Canta Yolanda?

Sí. Está cantando.

_____

4.

¿Canta Delia?

No. Está subiendo las

escaleras.

¡A leer!

Nombre _____

Read the following want ads and do the activity below.

A **HOSPITAL CENTRAL** *Se solicitan* Enfermeras y enfermeros • Con especialidad en terapia • Para trabajar por turnos de día y turnos de noche Teléfono 3126104 Sr. Raúl Silvestre, Administrador	**C** *SE SOLICITAN* **PINTORES** Trabajo inmediato No se requiere experiencia Avenida Aragua con Calle Mijares **MUEBLES ÚNICOS**
B **¡¡¡URGENTE!!!** Compañía internacional solicita personal administrativo, con más de 25 años, para diferentes actividades. Medio tiempo o completo. Llamar Sra. de Guzmán, 5731134	**D** **FÁBRICA DE MOTORES** Se solicitan obreros con experiencia. • Horarios mixtos • Beneficios fantásticos • Servicio médico • Semana de cinco (5) días Interesados presentarse en nuestra fábrica de lunes a viernes de 7:45 A.M. a 3:00 P.M.

Underline the words you know in these want ads. Then circle the words whose meanings you can guess. (No fair looking them up in the dictionary!) Next to each picture, write the letter of the ad that would best fit each person.

B _____

C _____

A _____

D _____

Extension: Have the class compare help-wanted ads in English and Spanish to point out phrases and words that are similar.

Nombre _____

Conexión con los estudios sociales

Try to match each of these people with their profession. Remember that words for verbs and professions are often related.

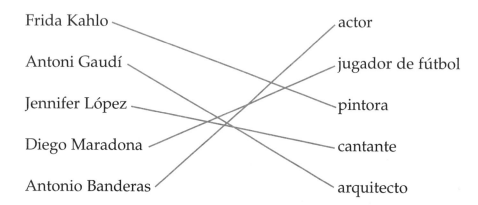

Frida Kahlo   actor

Antoni Gaudí   jugador de fútbol

Jennifer López   pintora

Diego Maradona   cantante

Antonio Banderas   arquitecto

Now choose three of the people and draw them doing something typical of their job. Write captions underneath, using *estar* and the activity they are doing.

_____   _____   _____

_____   _____   _____

Answers will vary.

Extension: Ask students about other people from the Spanish-speaking world they know. Write their names and occupations on the board.

⚙ ¡APRENDE MÁS! ⚙   Nombre _____

Spanish, French, Italian, and English have many words in common. If you know a word in English, you can often guess the meaning of a similar word in one of the Romance languages. Words that have similar spellings and meanings in different languages are called cognates.

How sharp are your detective skills? Look at the words in the following lists of professions. Observe how the words are spelled in French, Italian, and Spanish. Then write the English cognate on the line in the fourth column. The first one has been done for you.

French	Italian	Spanish	English
architecte	architetto	arquitecto	architect
artiste	artista	artista	artist
dentiste	dentista	dentista	dentist
soldat	soldato	soldado	soldier
peintre	pittore	pintor	painter
pilote	pilota	piloto	pilot
juge	giudice	juez	judge
athlète	atleta	atleta	athlete
directeur	direttore	director	director
musicien	musicista	músico	musician

¡A DIVERTIRSE!
Adivina la carrera

Nombre _____

For "Career Day," many visitors have turned up. You are in charge of passing out name tags. Use your detective skills to match each visitor to a card. Draw a line to match each card to the right picture.

Extension: Tell students that a dictionary should be their very last resort. They should try their skills of recognizing cognates and guessing by process of elimination first.

Andrés Antares, PLOMERO

María Sucre, VETERINARIA

Luisa Valle, REPORTERA

Pancho Corral, VAQUERO

Guillermo Ruiz, FOTÓGRAFO

Andrea Ballesteros, GUARDIA

¿Cómo se dice?

Textbook pages 66–69

Nombre _____

A. What can you see when you walk around the city? Underline the words that are NOT things you usually see on the street.

la gasolinera

la avenida

el paciente

la calle

los semáforos

la computadora

la farmacia

la parada del autobús

el taxista

el equipo

el coche

B. One of your friends wants her relatives to experience different ways of seeing the city. What does she suggest? Complete each question according to the picture.

1.  ¿Vamos _____ en autobús _____?

2. ¿Vamos _____ en taxi _____?

3. ¿Vamos _____ en coche _____?

4.  ¿Vamos _____ a pie _____?

¿Cómo se dice?

Textbook pages 70–74

Nombre _____

A. You are walking downtown. What can you see around you? Write the correct words next to the numbers on the list. Below, write the names of other things you can see in the picture.

M 1. **una plaza** _____

2. un teatro _____

3. un estacionamiento _____

4. un mercado _____

5. un rascacielos _____

6. unos edificios _____

una parada de autobús _____

unos coches, unos taxis, una farmacia, etc. Accept reasonable answers.

_____

_____

_____

Extension: Ask students what they would call this area of the city ("el centro").

¿Cómo se dice?

Textbook pages 75–79

Nombre _____

○ **A.** You are playing a video game in which you have to find the parking lot in a strange city. Your only guide is a computer voice. Complete each instruction it gives you by using the right form of the word in parentheses.

Ⓜ _____ **Camina** _____ por la plaza.
(caminar)

Ⓜ _____ **Corre** _____ al rascacielos.
(correr)

1. _____ Abre _____ la puerta del rascacielos.
(abrir)

2. _____ Sube _____ las escaleras.
(subir)

3. Si no hay un mapa, _____ baja _____ las escaleras.
(bajar)

4. _____ Busca _____ la farmacia.
(buscar)

5. _____ Compra _____ un mapa en la farmacia.
(comprar)

6. _____ Lee _____ el mapa en la plaza.
(leer)

7. _____ Camina _____ al mercado.
(caminar)

8. _____ Corre _____ al estacionamiento. ¡Muy bien!
(correr)

Nombre _____

B. Germán is the bossiest person in school. Write the orders he gives you today.

M escribir / tu nombre

¡**Escribe tu nombre!**

1. pintar / mi retrato

¡Pinta mi retrato!

2. recoger / mis libros

¡Recoge mis libros!

3. comer / tu sándwich

¡Come tu sándwich!

4. abrir / las ventanas

¡Abre las ventanas!

5. contestar / mis preguntas

¡Contesta mis preguntas!

C. You have decided to teach Germán some manners. It's your turn to give him some instructions. Use *por favor* to write six polite instructions, different from the ones above.

M Abre el buzón, por favor.

1. Sentences will vary. _____

2. _____

3. _____

4. _____

5. _____

6. _____

¿Cómo se dice?

Nombre _____

Textbook pages 80–83

○ **A.** Choose the correct answer for each situation. Follow the model.

M ¿Qué _____ tu mamá el día de tu cumpleaños?

   (a.) sirve

   b. servimos

1. ¿Qué _____ tus papás el día de *Thanksgiving?*

   (a.) sirven

   b. servimos

2. ¿Qué _____ a tus amigos para desayunar?

   a. sirvo

   (b.) sirves

3. El camarero _____ la sopa.

   (a.) sirve

   b. sirvo

4. ¿Qué _____ tú para comer en tu restaurante favorito?

   a. pido

   (b.) pides

5. Mi papá siempre _____ ensalada de cena.

   a. piden

   (b.) pide

6. Mis hermanos y yo siempre _____ helado en la playa.

   (a.) pedimos

   b. piden

7. Yo siempre _____ a mi hermana mayor por la calle.

   a. sigues

   (b.) sigo

8. Paula y yo _____ al maestro.

   a. siguen

   (b.) seguimos

Nombre _____

B. What do you and your family order in a restaurant? What do you serve for breakfast or lunch? Use the lists and the model to write sentences about your family's likes.

Mi padre	pedimos...
Yo	sirven...
Yo y mi hermana	piden...
Mis hermanos	pides...
Mi madre	pido...
Tú	sirvo...
Ustedes	pide...

M <u>Mi padre pide siempre pollo para comer.</u>

1. <u>Answers will vary.</u>

2. _____

3. _____

4. _____

5. _____

6. _____

C. Answer these questions.

M ¿Qué sirves en casa cuando hay amigos? _____ **Sirvo chocolate.**

1. ¿Qué pides el día de tu cumpleaños de cena? _____ Answers will vary.

2. ¿Qué pide tu mamá en el restaurante? _____

3. ¿Qué piden tus hermanos y tú en verano de almuerzo? _____

4. ¿Qué sirven en tu casa de cena? _____

¡A leer!

Nombre _____

Read the following paragraphs and answer the questions.

El buffet

En muchos hoteles, sirven un buffet. Es la mesa donde las personas se sirven todas las cosas que quieren de platos diferentes y deciden dónde sentarse. Es también una buena solución para los cumpleaños y otras comidas. Tienes que ofrecer distintos platos. Pero no tienes el problema de saber poner los cubiertos junto al plato, a la derecha (cuchara y cuchillos) y a la izquierda (tenedores), por ejemplo.

Pon los platos al principio y al final de la mesa. Todo tiene que estar bien caliente antes de servirlo, por supuesto. Y pon cucharas de servir para cada plato. El día antes, compra muchas servilletas y vasos de papel, ¡para limpiar menos en la cocina!

Draw a place setting, as described in the second paragraph. Label each item on your drawing. ▶

Make a drawing of a buffet table. Include as many details as you can, based on the description above. Label the details with phrases from the above reading. ⬇

Nombre _____

Conexión con las ciencias

Do you remember the names of planets in Spanish? What about the order they're in? Look at this picture and label the planets. Then color the planets.

Here are some clues:

El más grande es Júpiter.

El que está más cerca del Sol es Mercurio.

El que está más lejos del Sol es Plutón.

El que está más cerca de la Tierra es Venus.

Marte está entre la Tierra y Júpiter.

Saturno está entre Júpiter y Urano.

Neptuno está entre Plutón y Urano.

Expresa tus ideas

Nombre _____

Srta. Aventura and members of the Explorers' Club are starting out in the parking lot. Each person wants to do something different. Choose three club members and write instructions for each.

Before you assign this activity, you may wish to ask volunteers to point out places on the map. Then, ask advanced students to give one another directions to a place on the map.

BERTA: Quiero comprar frutas en el mercado. ¿Dónde está?

PACO: Tengo dolor de cabeza. ¿Dónde está la farmacia?

LUIS: Mi primo está en el hospital. ¿Dónde está el hospital?

RITA: ¿Dónde compro ropa nueva?

JOSÉ: ¡Tengo hambre! ¿Adónde voy?

PEPE: Quiero jugar a los juegos electrónicos. ¿Hay juegos en la ciudad?

ANA: Quiero ir al teatro y luego quiero ir al cine. ¿Dónde están?

| Hospital central | A la Moda (tienda de ropa) | Almacén Zamora | **Calle Monte** | Edificio Trujillo (rascacielos) | Farmacia Miraflores |

Avenida Bella

| Estación de bomberos | **Calle Miranda** | Teatro municipal | **Calle Torres** | Plaza de la Paz | **Calle Comercio** | Parada de autobuses |
| | | | | | | Compañía Aventura |

Avenida San Mateo

| Escuela secundaria Bolívar | Restaurante Hidalgo | La Casa Mágica (juegos electrónicos) | Cine Millonario | Estación de policía |

Avenida de la Fortuna

| **X** el estacionamiento | Tienda de animales | Taxis | Fábrica | **Calle Corto** Gasolinera | **Calle Milán** Mercado Poblano |

_____

_____

_____

_____

_____

_____

_____

Ask volunteers to read their sentences aloud.

◉ ¡A DIVERTIRSE! ◉

Nombre _____

Un rompecabezas

Read the descriptions and write the words in the blanks. Use the numbers to discover the safety tip.

1. Muchos vendedores venden frutas y otras cosas. Puedes comprar mucho aquí.
¿Qué es?

el $\frac{m}{1}$ $\frac{e}{2}$ $\frac{r}{3}$ $\frac{c}{4}$ $\frac{a}{5}$ $\frac{d}{6}$ $\frac{o}{7}$

2. Las personas compran gasolina para los coches aquí. ¿Qué es?

la $\frac{g}{8}$ $\frac{a}{9}$ $\frac{s}{10}$ $\frac{o}{11}$ $\frac{l}{12}$ $\frac{i}{13}$ $\frac{n}{14}$ $\frac{e}{15}$ $\frac{r}{16}$ $\frac{a}{17}$

3. Es un edificio muy alto. Hay muchos en las ciudades grandes. ¿Qué es?

el $\frac{r}{18}$ $\frac{a}{19}$ $\frac{s}{20}$ $\frac{c}{21}$ $\frac{a}{22}$ $\frac{c}{23}$ $\frac{i}{24}$ $\frac{e}{25}$ $\frac{l}{26}$ $\frac{o}{27}$ $\frac{s}{28}$

4. Las personas suben al autobús aquí. A veces bajan del autobús aquí. ¿Qué es?

la $\frac{p}{29}$ $\frac{a}{30}$ $\frac{r}{31}$ $\frac{a}{32}$ $\frac{d}{33}$ $\frac{a}{34}$ $\frac{d}{35}$ $\frac{e}{36}$

$\frac{a}{37}$ $\frac{u}{38}$ $\frac{t}{39}$ $\frac{o}{40}$ $\frac{b}{41}$ $\frac{ú}{42}$ $\frac{s}{43}$

¿Qué tienes que hacer al subir a un automóvil? Es muy importante.

$\frac{a}{5}$ $\frac{b}{41}$ $\frac{r}{31}$ $\frac{o}{7}$ $\frac{c}{23}$ h $\frac{a}{9}$ $\frac{r}{3}$ $\frac{t}{39}$ $\frac{e}{25}$ $\frac{e}{36}$ $\frac{l}{26}$

$\frac{c}{21}$ $\frac{i}{13}$ $\frac{n}{14}$ $\frac{t}{39}$ $\frac{u}{38}$ $\frac{r}{18}$ $\frac{ó}{40}$ $\frac{n}{14}$

Nombre _____

A. Srta. Canseco doesn't know much about sports and games. Use the pictures to answer her questions.

M

¿A qué juega Diego?

Juega al ajedrez. _____

1.

¿A qué juegan Jorge y Sara?

Juegan al volibol. _____

2.

¿A qué juega Teresa?

Juega al tenis. _____

3.

¿A qué juegan Mario y Paco?

Juegan al dominó. _____

4.

¿A qué juega Juanita?

Juega al béisbol. _____

Extension: Continue by asking students if they and their friends play the games and sports in the pictures (for example, **¿Tus amigos y tú juegan al ajedrez?**).

Nombre _____

B. Whom do you know in the neighborhood? Little Horacio is curious. Complete the sentences with the correct form of *conocer* to answer his questions.

M

¿___**Conoces**___ al Sr. Trujillo?

¡Claro que sí! También ___**conozco**___ a su hija Mariela.

1.

¿Tus hermanos ___**conocen**___ a Luisito?

¡Claro que sí! También ___**conocen**___ a su hermana Mónica.

2.

¿___**Conoces**___ a Flora?

¡Claro que sí! También ___**conozco**___ a su primo Federico.

3.

¿Tus amigos y tú ___**conocen**___ a Samuel?

¡Claro que sí! También ___**conocemos**___ a su primo Eduardo.

4.

¿Tu mamá ___**conoce**___ a Dolores?

¡Claro que sí! También ___**conoce**___ a su hermanito Diego.

Extension: Reuse the page to ask questions about the people and activities in the pictures (for example, ¿Qué hace el Sr. Trujillo? ¿Como as el Sr. Trujillo? ¿Es alto? ¿Es delgado?).

Nombre _____

C. You want someone to go to the movies with you. Everyone is busy at the moment. What do they say they are doing when you ask them to go?

Students' answers may vary. Accept reasonable responses.

 Adela, ¿quieres ir al cine?

No puedo ahora. Estoy barriendo el piso.

1.  Ricardo, ¿quieres ir al cine?

No puedo ahora. Estoy poniendo la mesa.

2.  Diana, ¿quieres ir al cine?

No puedo ahora. Estoy subiendo las escaleras.

3.  Papá, ¿quieres ir al cine?

No puedo ahora. Estoy escribiendo un libro.

4.  Pancho, ¿quieres ir al cine?

No puedo ahora. Estoy comiendo una manzana.

Extension: Continue by asking questions (for example, ¿Qué hace Adela? / Ella barre el piso.).

Nombre _____

D. You are describing different people in your classroom, including yourself. Be sure to use the correct form of *ser* to complete each sentence.

Ⓜ Ramón _____ **es** _____ muy inteligente.

1. Mabel y Rogelio _____ **son** _____ muy generosos.

2. María _____ **es** _____ muy atlética.

3. Felipe y yo no _____ **somos** _____ altos.

4. Graciela _____ **es** _____ muy tímida.

5. Francisco y Luisa _____ **son** _____ populares.

6. Yo no _____ **soy** _____ muy _____ **Answers will vary.** _____.

E. Cecilia is very curious about your family. And you love talking about them. How will you describe them? Finish the sentences that are appropriate for your family. You can describe their personality or their physical traits. Use the verb *ser.*

Be sensitive to the fact that not all students may have siblings. Ask them to come up with a different relative or friend instead.

Ⓜ Mi mamá _____ **es alta y generosa** _____.

1. Mi hermano _____ **Answers will vary.** _____.

2. Mi hermana _____.

3. Mi padre _____.

4. Mi papá y mi mamá _____.

5. Mis hermanos _____.

6. Mi hermano y yo _____.

7. Mi hermana y yo _____.

8. Mis hermanos y yo _____.

Nombre _____

F. These people are lost in town. Complete the dialogues and give them directions. Use the verbs in brackets.

M ¿Dónde está la calle Peral?

_____**Sigue**_____ (seguir) derecho y _____**dobla**_____ (dobla) a la derecha.

1. ¿Dónde está la farmacia?

_____Sigue_____ (seguir) derecho y _____dobla_____ (doblar) a la izquierda.

2. ¿Dónde está la plaza?

_____Sigue_____ (seguir) derecho.

3. ¿Dónde está la parada de autobús?

_____Dobla_____ (doblar) a la izquierda, luego _____dobla_____ (doblar) a la derecha y ahí está.

G. You need to ask your friend to do some things. But be polite! Write commands using the imperative, and remember to use *por favor.*

M escribir _____**Escribe tu nombre, por favor.**_____

1. comer _____come, answers will vary._____

2. abrir _____abre, answers will vary._____

3. correr _____corre, answers will vary._____

4. recoger _____recoge, answers will vary._____

5. pintar _____pinta, answers will vary._____

Nombre _____

H. Paula and Ricardo are talking about food they like, what they do when they eat out and what their families eat. Complete their conversation using *servir* and *pedir* in the correct form.

PAULA: Siempre _____**pido**_____ pollo cuando voy al restaurante.

RICARDO: A mí también me gusta, pero yo siempre _____**pido**_____ pescado.

PAULA: Mis papás también siempre _____**piden**_____ pescado.

RICARDO: Mis también siempre _____**piden**_____ pollo, como tú.

PAULA: Mi mamá siempre _____**sirve**_____ pollo los domingos en casa.

RICARDO: Mi mamá _____**sirve**_____ arroz los domingos. ¿Qué

_____**sirven**_____ en tu casa el día de Acción de Gracias?

PAOLA: __**Sirven** *or* **Servimos**__ pavo, arroz y guisantes.

RICARDO: Mis abuelos también _____**sirven**_____ pavo. Siempre comemos en su casa el Día de Acción de Gracias.

PAOLA: Y mi papá siempre _____**sirve**_____ el café.

RICARDO: En mi casa, mis hermanos y yo _____**servimos**_____ el café.

¿Cómo se dice?

Nombre _____

Textbook pages 88–91

○ **A.** What places and forms of transportation can you see in a city? Unscramble the letters and write the correct letter next to each name.

M le utrpeo ___el puerto___ A

1. el nviaó ___el avión___ B

2. le rbaoc ___el barco___ A

3. la esacntió ed rntese ___la estación de trenes___ C

4. le aeerpurtoo ___el aeropuerto___ B

5. el ntre ___el tren___ C

A 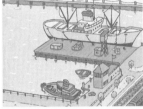 B  C

¡Piénsalo!

See how quickly you can answer these questions.

¿Dónde hay barcos?

___En el puerto.___

¿Dónde hay aviones?

___En el aeropuerto.___

¿Dónde hay trenes?

___En la estación de trenes.___

¿Cómo se dice?

Textbook pages 92–95

Nombre _____

A. Geography has always been one of your best subjects. Use the phrases in the list to complete the sentences telling where each country is located.

América del Norte   América Central   Europa   América del Sur

M Bolivia es un país de _____ **América del Sur** _____.

1. Panamá es un país de _____ América Central _____.

2. España es un país de _____ Europa _____.

3. Honduras es un país de _____ América Central _____.

4. Chile es un país de _____ América del Sur _____.

5. Estados Unidos es un país de _____ América del Norte _____.

6. Portugal es un país de _____ Europa _____.

7. Colombia es un país de _____ América del Sur _____.

8. Venezuela es un país de _____ América del Sur _____.

9. Canadá es un país de _____ América del Norte _____.

10. Costa Rica es un país de _____ América Central _____.

You may want to display a map of the American and European continents for this exercise.

¡Piénsalo!

Circle the country that doesn't belong.

1. Cuba

República Dominicana

Puerto Rico

Bolivia

2. España

Argentina

Perú

Ecuador

Nombre _____

● **B.** Your class has prepared a map of Central America, South America and the Caribbean, but you have run out of vowel cards. You will have to write vowels by hand. Fill in the missing vowels, and then circle the sections of the map with different colors as follows:

América del Sur = verde

América Central = rojo

El Caribe = azul

A RG E NT I N A   C O ST A   R I C A

B O L I V I A   G U A T E M A L A

CH I L E   H O ND U R A S

C O L O MB I A   N I C A R A G U A

E C U A D O R   P A N A M A

P A R A G U A Y   E L   S A LV A D O R

P E R U   C U B A

U R U G U A Y   P U E RT O   R I C O

V E N E Z U E L A   R E P U B L I C A

B E L I C E   D O M I N I C A N A

¿Cómo se dice?

Nombre _____

Textbook pages 96–99

A. Your teacher has asked you to write a report on nationalities. Complete each sentence with the correct nationality.

M Las personas que viven en Puerto Rico son ___**puertorriqueñas**___.

1. Las personas que viven en Ecuador son ___**ecuatorianas**___.

2. Las personas que viven en Chile son ___**chilenas**___.

3. Las personas que viven en Panamá son ___**panameñas**___.

4. Las personas que viven en Nicaragua son ___**nicaragüenses**___.

5. Las personas que viven en México son ___**mexicanas**___.

B. Sr. Figueroa wants to check if everyone has been paying attention. How well can you do on his "quickie quiz"? Use the information about where everyone is from to give their correct nationalities.

M Migdalia es de Guatemala. Ella es ___**guatemalteca**___.

1. Pierre es de Haití. Él es ___**haitiano**___.

2. Nélida es de Perú. Ella es ___**peruana**___.

3. Tania y Patricia son de Uruguay. Ellas son ___**uruguayas**___.

4. Óscar y Martín son de Costa Rica. Ellos son ___**costarricenses**___.

¿Cómo se dice?

Nombre _____

A. Susana has created some rebus puzzles for you to solve. Look at the words and pictures, and then write the complete sentence on the line provided.

You may want to suggest that students look at the map on page 49 in order to recognize maps of different countries.

M Luis va a

1. Margarita va a

2. Javier va a

3. Irene va a

4. Yo voy a

M _____ **Luis va a España en avión.**

1. _____ Margarita va a México en coche.

2. _____ Javier va a Perú en barco.

3. _____ Irene va a Panamá en tren.

4. _____ Yo voy a la escuela en bicicleta.

Nombre _____

B. **What form of transportation do you take for short distances? What kind of transportation will you take for long distances? Answer each question according to what you think is the best method of transportation.**

M ¿Cómo vas al mercado?

Voy al mercado en autobús.

1. ¿Cómo vas a Europa?

Answers will vary.

2. ¿Cómo vas al centro de tu ciudad?

_____

3. ¿Cómo vas a México?

_____

4. ¿Cómo vas a la República Dominicana?

_____

5. ¿Cómo vas a la escuela por la mañana?

_____

6. ¿Cómo vas a América del Sur?

_____

¡Piénsalo!

Match the picture to its label and then answer the question below.

Un burro    Una nave espacial

¿Cómo vas a otro planeta: en burro o en nave espacial?

Voy a otro planeta en nave espacial.

¡A leer!

Nombre _____

Read this paragraph and do the activity below.

Desiertos misteriosos

Tres de los lugares más misteriosos del mundo son los desiertos de Nazca, Atacama y Pisco. Los tres lugares están en la costa sudamericana del océano Pacífico, entre Perú y Chile. En su arena hay dibujadas figuras muy grandes.

En el desierto de Atacama, en Chile, hay un gigante de 120 metros en la arena. Sólo podemos ver el gigante desde un avión o helicóptero. En Pisco, en el desierto peruano de Paracas, hay un candelabro muy grande, de casi 200 metros. En el desierto de Nazca, en Perú, entre los Andes y el océano Pacífico, hay cientos de líneas rectas, dibujos geométricos y figuras de animales.

> Nota:
> **Desierto** means "desert."
> **Arena** means "sand."
> **Candelabro** means "candelabra (complex candlestick)."

Match the names of the places with the pictures, according to the text you just read. Under each one, write the name of the country where it is found.

Atacama   Pisco   Nazca

_____ Chile _____   _____ Peru _____   _____ Peru _____

Nombre _____

Conexión con las matemáticas

Look at this pie chart. It represents different groups of foreign-born Spanish speakers who live in the United States. Use the information below to label each wedge of the pie with the group it represents. Then write sentences telling how many people from each country live in the United States.

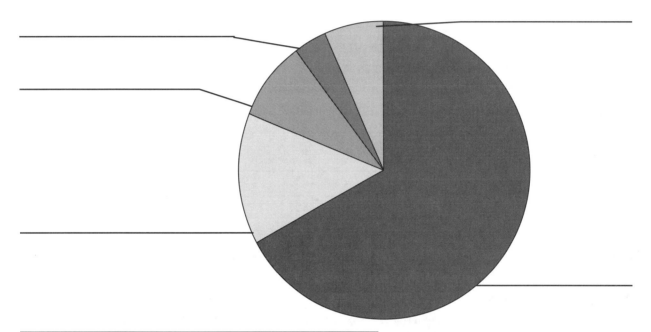

otros 1 millón
puertorriqueños 1.3 millones
centroamericanos y sudamericanos 2.2 millones
cubanos 577,000 millones
mexicanos 10.4 millones

Source: U.S. Census

66.9%: mexicanos
14.3%: centroamericanos y sudamericanos
8.6%: puertorriqueños
3.7%: cubanos
6.5%: otros

_____

_____

_____

_____

≈ ¡APRENDE MÁS! ≈

Nombre _____

Have you ever borrowed anything from a friend? Languages sometimes take some words they need from other languages. These words are called **loan words.**

One reason languages borrow words is that they need to express something they cannot express with the words they already have. This may happen because the word refers to a new or imported object or concept. Languages come into contact with each other through trade and travel, and lend and borrow words from each other. Sometimes these words are adopted exactly as they are spelled in the original language, and sometimes they are adapted.

Here is a list of words that Spanish has borrowed from English. Can you find the English original?

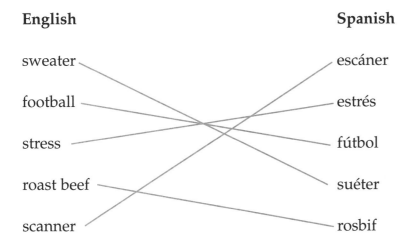

English	Spanish
sweater	escáner
football	estrés
stress	fútbol
roast beef	suéter
scanner	rosbif

Here is a list of words that English has borrowed from Spanish. Can you find the Spanish original?

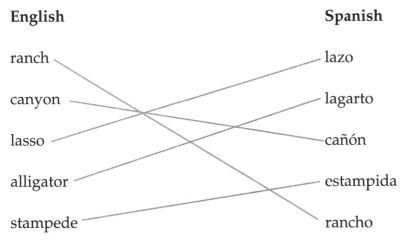

English	Spanish
ranch	lazo
canyon	lagarto
lasso	cañón
alligator	estampida
stampede	rancho

¡A DIVERTIRSE!

Nombre _____

Un juego internacional

In the column on the left are the names of countries. In the column of the right are the names of capital cities. How many capital cities do you know without looking at a map? Write the letter of the capital city on the line next to its country.

__h__ Bolivia		**a.** Madrid
__f__ Nicaragua		**b.** México, D.F.
__a__ España		**c.** Caracas
__l__ Panamá		**d.** Santiago
__j__ República Dominicana		**e.** Lima
__g__ Paraguay		**f.** Managua
__d__ Chile		**g.** Asunción
__c__ Venezuela		**h.** La Paz
__e__ Perú		**i.** La Habana
__b__ México		**j.** Santo Domingo
__i__ Cuba		**k.** Buenos Aires
__k__ Argentina		**l.** Panamá

¿Cómo se dice?

Textbook pages 108–111

Nombre _____

A. You are helping your grandfather plan a trip. Use the list to complete the sentences about your grandfather's trip planning.

un billete   un viajero   ✓viajar   descansar

la agente   pagar   la agencia   costar

M Mi abuelo piensa ____viajar____ muy lejos.

1. Mi abuelo viaja mucho. Es ____un viajero____ con mucha experiencia.

2. Primero, tenemos que ir a ____la agencia____ de viajes.

3. A ____la agente____ de viajes le gusta ayudar a las personas.

4. Abuelito tiene que comprar ____un billete____.

5. Va a ____costar____ muchos dólares.

6. Mi abuelo tiene que ____pagar____ trescientos dólares.

7. ¡Pero sabe que va a poder ____descansar____ mucho en su viaje!

B. You are planning a trip. Write four questions to ask your travel agent.

M ¿Es bonito México?

¿Va a costar mucho el billete?

1. ____Students' questions will vary.____

2. _____

3. _____

4. _____

Extension: Have students choose partners to ask and answer one another's questions.

¿Cómo se dice?

Nombre _____

Textbook pages 112–116

○ **A.** Your family is planning to take a trip to go on vacation this winter. Where do family members want to go? Use the pictures as clues to see how they answer your questions.

Emilio, ¿adónde quieres ir?

Quiero ir a la selva.

1.

Cecilia, ¿adónde quieres ir?

Quiero ir al desierto.

2.

Ramón y Tania, ¿adónde quieren ir?

Queremos ir al valle.

3.

Abuelita, ¿adónde quieres ir?

Quiero ir a la playa.

4.

Mamá y papá, ¿adónde quieren ir?

Queremos ir a las montañas.

¿Cómo se dice?

Nombre _____

Textbook pages 117–121

○ **A.** Elena is back from her vacation and is showing you her photo album. She took some notes to write captions under each picture. Choose the right words for each picture and write the caption for her.

1. Yo / nadar / en la playa / todos los días

2. Mis hermanos / montar a caballo

3. Mis papás / leer libros

4. Mi mamá / pintar cuadros

5. Mi papá / sacar fotos

6. Nosotros / subir montañas / a veces

M

Mis hermanos montan a caballo.

Nosotros subimos montañas a veces.

Yo nado en la playa todos los días.

Mis papás leen libros.

Mi papá saca fotos.

Mi mamá pinta cuadros.

Nombre _____

C. Enrique has written a paragraph about his favorite aunt, who is a photographer *(fotógrafa)*. Help him finish it. Complete each sentence using the correct form of the verb in parentheses.

You may wish to use this exercise for dictation practice.

Mi tía Adriana

Mi tía Adriana _____**es**_____ fotógrafa. Ella _____**va**_____ a muchos
            (ser)   (ir)

países para sacar fotos. Ahora ella _____**está**_____ en el Atacama, un desierto en
                                            (estar)

Chile. Yo _____**soy**_____ fotógrafo también. Algunas veces mi tía y yo
               (ser)

_____**vamos**_____ al río. Otras veces _____**vamos**_____ a una ciudad. Todos
     (ir)   (ir)

los amigos de mi tía _____**son**_____ fotógrafos. Ahora, dos amigos
                            (ser)

_____**están**_____ en Costa Rica. Ellos siempre _____**van**_____ a las selvas
     (estar)   (ir)

en el otoño. El trabajo de los fotógrafos _____**es**_____ muy interesante.
                                      (ser)

Extension: Have students write questions to ask Enrique and his aunt Adriana.

¿Cómo se dice?

Nombre _____

Textbook pages 122–125

○ **A.** Your neighbor Pepito asks many questions. Maybe someday he'll become a detective! Use the words in parentheses to complete his questions.

M (poder)　　¿Cuándo _____**puedes**_____ tú viajar?

1. (almorzar)　¿Dónde _____almuerzan_____ tus amigos y tú?

2. (volver)　　¿A qué hora _____vuelven_____ tus hermanos?

3. (poder)　　¿_____Puedo_____ yo correr en la casa?

4. (probar)　　¿_____Prueban_____ tus amigos los platos tropicales?

5. (costar)　　¿Cuánto _____cuesta_____ un billete a Canadá?

◑ **B.** Now you can answer some of Pepito's questions. Answer Pepito's questions in Exercise A using the words in parentheses in this exercise.

M (en el verano)　　**Puedo viajar en el verano.**

1. (en el comedor)　Almorzamos en el comedor.

2. (a las cuatro)　　Mis hermanos vuelven a las cuatro.

3. (no / en la casa)　No puedes correr en la casa.

4. (a veces)　　　　A veces prueban platos tropicales.

5. (muchos dólares)　Un billete cuesta muchos dólares.

Nombre _____

C. Inés and her friends are practicing their comedy skits for the talent show. Help them out when they forget a word. Complete their conversations using the correct form of a verb from the list.

estar	cerrar	ser
comenzar	pensar	costar

M INÉS: La clase de matemáticas __comienza__ en quince minutos.

¡Y nosotros __estamos__ muy lejos de la escuela!

1. HUGO: ¿Qué __piensas__ hacer? ¡La clase __comienza__ en cinco minutos!

INÉS: ¡__Pienso__ correr mucho!

2. PAPÁ: ¿Por qué __cierran__ las ventanas, chicos? Hace calor.

NIÑO: __Cerramos__ las ventanas porque hay un pájaro muy grande en el patio.

PAPÁ: ¡Hijos! No __es__ un pájaro. ¡__Es__ el nuevo sombrero de mamá!

3. HOMBRE: ¿Dónde __piensan__ ustedes pasar las vacaciones?

MUJER: __Pensamos__ viajar a Colombia, a España, a Puerto Rico y a México.

HOMBRE: ¡Uy! ¿__Cuestan__ mucho los billetes?

MUJER: ¿Qué billetes? __Pensamos__ ir al cine todos los días.

¡A leer!

Nombre _____

Read these paragraphs and answer the questions.

Otros lugares misteriosos de América Latina

En México

Teotihuacán. El centro religioso más importante de la América precolombina. Construido con cálculos astronómicos exactos.

Palenque. El lugar elegido por los mayas para estudiar el cielo. Está en el estado mexicano de Chiapas.

En Costa Rica

Isla del Coco. Dicen que en esta isla costarricense hay tres tesoros de piratas.

En Colombia

Lago Guatavita. Dicen que El Dorado, la leyenda de los españoles, está en el lago Guatavita, a 50 kilómetros de Bogotá, la capital colombiana.

En Perú

Machu Picchu. Son templos, palacios y observatorios incas; están en las montañas de Los Andes.

1. ¿Qué lugares misteriosos podemos visitar en América Latina?

   Teotihuacán, Palenque, el lago Guatavita, la isla del Coco, Machu Picchu, etc.

2. ¿Dónde está Palenque?

   Palenque está en México, en el estado de Chiapas.

3. ¿Qué es Chiapas?

   Chiapas es el nombre de un estado mexicano.

4. ¿Está lejos el lago Guatavita de la capital de Colombia?

   No, está a 50 kilómetros de Bogotá.

5. ¿Dónde está la isla del Coco? ¿Qué hay en la isla?

   La isla del Coco está en Costa Rica. Dicen que hay tres tesoros de piratas.

6. ¿Dónde está Machu Picchu?

   Machu Picchu está en Perú, en los Andes.

Nombre _____

Conexión con los estudios sociales

Make a map of your ideal vacation destination. First, draw the outline of your imaginary country. Then make a map key and add symbols for all the different fun places you will add to it, such as beaches, volcanoes, lakes, mountains, etc.

Now write a promotional paragraph saying why this is the ideal vacation destination. Include the cost of tickets, the sights people can see, things they can do, etc.

You may choose to show the students the following example:

Viaja a Maravilandia. En Maravilandia puedes descansar, visitar la selva...

_____

_____

_____

_____

Expresa tus ideas

Nombre _____

The Explorers' Club is back again! They are making plans for an exciting trip this year. Will they ever agree on a destination? Write at least five sentences based on the picture.

Students' sentences will vary. Possible sentences include: La Srta. Aventura piensa

ir a las montañas. Pepe y Ana piensan viajar a la selva. Hay pájaros exóticos en la

selva. José no quiere viajar al desierto. Rita piensa viajar a una ciudad grande.

Quiere ir a una fiesta en taxi. Luis piensa viajar en barco. Quiere ir al río. Berta no

quiere viajar a las montañas. No quiere estar cerca de un volcán. Paco sí piensa

viajar a las montañas. A él le gustan las niñas bonitas.

_____

_____

_____

 ¡A DIVERTIRSE! ⊚   Nombre _____

En busca del tesoro

Mario Ojos de Águila and his brave assistant Victoria Valiente are searching for the treasure of the enchanted emerald. They are lost and have radioed for your help. Lead them out of the rain forest to the enchanted emerald by tracing the correct route.

After students have traced the route to the treasure, have them describe the areas and modes of transportation on the way to the treasure. You may guide them by asking questions (for example, **¿Por dónde pasas primero? Luego, ¿adónde vas?**).

¿Cómo se dice?   Nombre _____

Textbook pages 130–133

A. You spent hours arranging the bulletin-board display. Overnight, someone removed all the labels from under the pictures! Match each label to a picture in order to rearrange the display. Write the correct name for each item or person.

el equipaje

el pasajero

la maleta

la piloto

el asistente de vuelo

la asistente de vuelo

los asientos

el horario

1. (la maleta)   4. (la asistente de vuelo)   7. (el pasajero)

2. (los asientos)   5. (el horario)   8. (el asistente de vuelo)

3. (la piloto)   6. (el equipaje)

¿Cómo se dice?

Nombre _____

Textbook pages 134–137

A. You love to go to the airport just to watch the people and activity. What do you observe? Use the list of words to complete the sentences.

hacer fila	los pilotos	✓ despega
vuela	aterriza	a tiempo
cómodos	los asistentes de vuelo	la maleta

M El avión sale del aeropuerto. El avión _____**despega**_____.

1. Otro avión llega al aeropuerto. Ese avión _____**aterriza**_____.

2. Antes de subir al avión, los pasajeros tienen que _____**hacer fila**_____.

3. Un vuelo no llega tarde y no llega temprano. Llega _____**a tiempo**_____.

4. _____**Los pilotos**_____ preparan los instrumentos del avión.

5. Dentro del avión, los pasajeros buscan los asientos más _____**cómodos**_____.

6. _____**Los asistentes de vuelo**_____ ayudan a los pasajeros.

B. Your friend Lucinda works at the airport, announcing the flight arrivals and departures. What is she announcing now? Write each sentence using *llega* or *sale.*

M (vuelo 93 / llegada: 11:15) _____**El vuelo 93 llega a las once y cuarto.**_____

1. (vuelo 22 / salida: 2:30) _____**El vuelo 22 sale a las dos y media.**_____

2. (vuelo 15 / salida: 6:30) _____**El vuelo 15 sale a las seis y media.**_____

3. (vuelo 32 / llegada 4:00) _____**El vuelo 32 llega a las cuatro.**_____

4. (vuelo 57 / llegada: 5:10) _____**El vuelo 57 llega a las cinco y diez.**_____

¿Cómo se dice?

Nombre _____

Textbook pages 138–141

A. Wilfredo forgot to eat breakfast this morning. He is impatient as he stands in line for lunch in the cafeteria. Who is in line ahead of him? Use the correct form of *hacer* to complete each question and answer.

M **P:** Luis, ¿_____ **hacen** _____ fila Lupe y José?

   R: Sí, ellos _____ **hacen** _____ fila.

1. **P:** Daniel, ¿_____ **haces** _____ fila?

    R: Sí, _____ **hago** _____ fila.

2. **P:** Elena, ¿_____ **hacen** _____ fila Carlota y tú?

    R: Sí, _____ **hacemos** _____ fila.

3. **P:** Sra. González, ¿_____ **hace** _____ fila usted?

    R: Sí, _____ **hago** _____ fila.

4. **P:** Paula y Blanca, ¿_____ **hacen** _____ fila ustedes?

    R: Sí, _____ **hacemos** _____ fila.

5. **P:** Francisco, ¿_____ **haces** _____ fila?

    R: Sí, yo _____ **hago** _____ fila también.

Wilfredo: ¡Caramba! ¡No voy a comer nunca!

Nombre _____

● **B.** Margarita has just received a letter from Lorenzo, her cousin who lives in Puerto Rico. What does he tell her? Read the letter, then answer the questions.

You may wish to use the letter for dictation practice.

Querida Margarita:

Saludos desde Puerto Rico. Hace muy buen tiempo en nuestra isla.

Mis padres y yo hacemos planes para viajar a España en diciembre. Pensamos ir a Madrid y a la Costa del Sol.

En enero, hago un viaje a Florida con mi clase. En enero, siempre hace sol en Florida. Nosotros hacemos planes para ir a las playas bonitas. No queremos ir a los parques de atracciones, porque no nos gusta hacer fila.

Con cariño,

Lorenzo

Help students guess the meaning of **parques de atracciones** (*amusement parks*) by naming parks with which the students are familiar (for example, **Six Flags es un parque de atracciones.**).
Enrichment: Students may use Lorenzo's letter as a model for writing their own letters about making plans and taking trips.

1. ¿Qué tiempo hace en Puerto Rico?

   Hace muy buen tiempo.

2. ¿Qué hacen Lorenzo y sus padres?

   Hacen planes para viajar a España (en diciembre).

3. ¿Adónde van a hacer un viaje?

   Van a hacer un viaje a Madrid y a la Costa del Sol.

4. ¿Qué hace Lorenzo en enero?

   Hace un viaje a Florida.

5. ¿Con quiénes va a hacer el viaje?

   Va a hacer el viaje con sus compañeros de clase.

6. ¿Qué planes hacen ellos?

   Hacen planes para ir a las playas (bonitas).

¿Cómo se dice?

Nombre _____

Textbook pages 142–145

A. Can you spot a liar? Can you tell when someone is telling the truth? Look at these people and read what they are saying. Then decide if they are telling *la verdad* or *una mentira.*

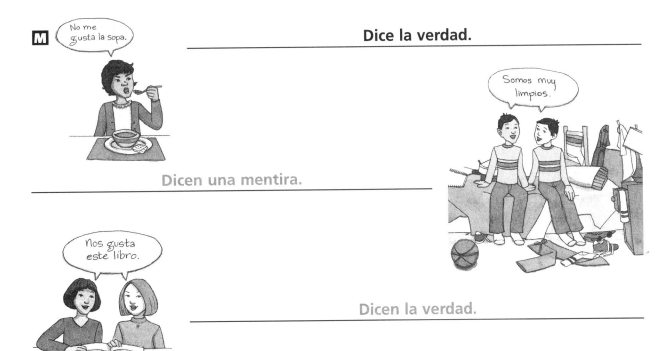

M *No me gusta la sopa.*

Dice la verdad.

Somos muy limpios.

Dicen una mentira.

Nos gusta este libro.

Dicen la verdad.

B. You are asking a lot of questions today! Look at the questions you've asked and the answers you got. Then tell someone else what the answers were.

Tú: ¿Podemos ir a la playa?

Tus amigos: No, más tarde.

Dicen que no.

Tú: ¿Puedo abrir la ventana?

Tu maestro: Sí, claro.

Dice que sí.

Tú: ¿Podemos ir al parque?

Tus papás: Sí, pueden ir.

Dicen que sí.

Tú: ¿Puede ir al baño?

La asistente de vuelo: No, ahora vamos a aterrizar.

Dice que no.

Nombre _____

C. It seems that every two minutes, someone is saying something to Felipe. Are you having a day like that, too? Write at least six sentences using words from each column. First look at Felipe's sentences to get some ideas.

mis papás	digo que	tener (examen, frío . . .)
el maestro	dices que	ir a (viajar, cantar . . .)
la maestra	dice que	ser (simpático, inteligente . . .)
mis amigos	decimos que	gustar (la película, la clase . . .)
yo	dicen que	tener que (estudiar, lavar . . .)
tú		hacer (frío, buen tiempo . . .)
nosotros		

M El maestro dice que tenemos que estudiar mucho.

Mis amigos dicen que no les gustan las películas largas.

Tú dices que hace muy mal tiempo hoy.

Yo digo que mis amigos son simpáticos.

You may wish to present additional models before assigning this exercise.

1. Sentences will vary. _____

2. _____

3. _____

4. _____

5. _____

6. _____

¡A leer!

Nombre _____

Read the following text and answer the questions.

Notas para el viajero

Podemos decir que en México el tren es un recuerdo, de noventa años atrás. Para viajar por un país de dos millones de kilómetros cuadrados, el viajero debe decidir entre el avión y el autobús. El autobús se llama también **camión** en México. Es muy necesario, porque el avión es caro, y cuesta unos 250 dólares por billete.

Pero en México viajar en autobús cuesta menos dinero que en otros países. Además, desde la ventana los pasajeros ven cactos, tierra árida, selva tropical, playas, bosques... Muchos de los viajes duran más de diez horas, con paradas frecuentes.

> Nota:
> **Recuerdo** means "memory."
> **Atrás** means "back."

Answers may vary. Possible answers are provided.

1. ¿Viajan mucho las personas en tren en México?

   No, en México no usan mucho el tren. Usan el autobús o el avión.

2. ¿En qué viajan más las personas en México: en autobús o en avión? ¿Por qué?

   En autobús. El autobús cuesta menos dinero que el avión.

3. ¿Cuesta mucho el billete de avión en México?

   El billete de avión cuesta mucho. Cuesta 250 dólares por billete.

5. ¿Cuántas horas duran algunos viajes en autobús?

   Más de diez horas.

6. ¿Hacen muchas paradas los autobuses?

   Sí, los autobuses hacen muchas paradas.

Nombre _____

Conexión con las matemáticas

There are 24 hours in a day, 60 minutes in an hour, and 60 seconds in a minute. Look at how long these people's flight planes took, and say which took longer. If they all left at the time shown, say at what time each arrived.

Phoenix—Bogotá, salida 2:30 P.M.

Laura: 5.5 horas _____ **Llega a las 8:00 P.M.** _____

Luis: 240 minutos _____ Llega a las 6:30 P.M. _____

Lidia: 16,200 segundos _____ Llega a las 6:00 P.M. _____

Caracas—Madrid, salida 8:00 P.M.

Sara: 10.5 horas _____ Llega a las 6:30 A.M. _____

Santi: 540 minutos _____ Llega a las 5:00 A.M. _____

Sandra: 36,000 segundos _____ Llega a las 6:00 A.M. _____

México, DF—Buenos Aires, salida 5:30 A.M.

Ramón: 5 horas _____ Llega a las 10:30 A.M. _____

Raquel: 300 minutos _____ Llega a las 10:30 A.M. _____

Rosa: 18,000 segundos _____ Llega a las 10:30 A.M. _____

Why don't you make some fun calculations? Find:

¿Cuántos segundos duermes al día? _____

¿Cuántos minutos estás en la escuela al día? _____

¿Cuántos segundos ves la televisión? _____

⊗ ¡APRENDE MÁS! ⊗

Nombre _____

Two different words that have the same, or almost the same, meaning are called synonyms. In Spanish, there are many words that have synonyms. For example, the words *avión* and *aeroplano* are synonyms. Study the following list of synonyms in Spanish.

Enrichment: If you have access to a dictionary of synonyms in Spanish, bring it to class. Students may enjoy finding synonyms for words they have learned.

La palabra	Los sinónimos
el billete	el boleto, el pasaje
el país	la nación, la patria
poner	colocar
la maleta	la valija
cómico	divertido, gracioso, chistoso
el compañero	el colega, el camarada
hacer (una cosa)	producir, fabricar
hablar	conversar, platicar
el coche	el auto, el carro
la asistente de vuelo	la aeromoza, la azafata

Read the following sentences. Find a synonym in the list above for each word in heavy black letters. Then rewrite the sentence, using the synonym.

La **asistente de vuelo pone** las **maletas** de los pasajeros debajo de los asientos.

La aeromoza (azafata) coloca las valijas de los pasajeros debajo de los asientos.

Mi **compañero** no quiere comprar **un billete**.

Mi colega (camarada) no quiere comprar un boleto (un pasaje).

Los obreros **hacen coches** en la fábrica.

Los obreros producen (fabrican) autos (carros) en la fábrica.

Me gusta **hablar** con las personas **cómicas**.

Me gusta conversar (platicar) con personas divertidas (graciosas, chistosas).

¡A DIVERTIRSE!

Nombre _____

Busca las palabras

First, read the sentences. Then look in the puzzle for each word in a sentence that is in heavy, **black** letters. The words may appear across, down, or diagonally. When you find a word, circle it. After you have circled all the words, you will find the name of a country that is noted for its coffee.

1. La **piloto** siempre tiene un **asiento cómodo.**

2. **Hago fila** con mis amigos.

3. La **pasajera viaja** con una **maleta** grande.

4. La asistente de vuelo **busca** la **salida** del vuelo en el horario.

5. ¿Tú **dices** que el avión **vuela** primero y **despega** luego? ¡Imposible!

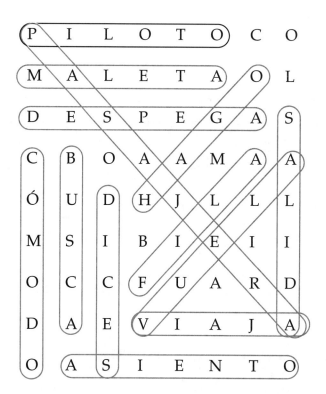

Colombia

_____ produce mucho café.

Nombre _____

A. Your key pal Sara has written you an e-mail to tell you about what she and her family do on their vacation, but she cannot remember the correct form of the verbs she wants to use. Help her out.

Mi familia y yo vamos de vacaciones a un pueblo pequeño en la montaña. Nos gusta

mucho. Mis hermanos y yo _____**nadamos**_____ (nadar) todos los días en el lago. Yo

también _____**leo**_____ (leer) mucho, especialmente libros de aventuras.

Muchos días _____**como/comemos**_____ (comer) bocadillos y ensalada cerca del lago. A

veces mis papás, mis hermanos y yo _____**subimos**_____ (subir) montañas y

entonces _____**comemos**_____ (comer) en la montaña. Mi mamá siempre

_____**saca**_____ (sacar) fotos. Mi papá no saca muchas fotos, a él le gusta pintar.

Por las tardes _____**pinta**_____ (pintar) en el jardín. Mi hermano pequeño

_____**monta**_____ (montar) a caballo, pero yo no. Tenemos muchos amigos y

muchos días nos _____**visitan**_____ (visitar) y _____**comen**_____ (comer) con

nosotros. A veces también mis abuelos _____**visitan**_____ (visitar) nuestra casa.

¿Y tú? ¿Qué haces en vacaciones? ¿Adónde vas? ¿_____**Nadas**_____ (nadar) en

la playa o en la piscina? ¿_____**Subes**_____ (subir) montañas?

¿_____**Visitas**_____ (visitar) a tus familiares?

Cuéntame todo.
Un beso,
Sara

B. Now, on another piece of paper, write your reply to Sara's e-mail. Be sure to answer all her questions!

Nombre _____

C. Sr. Rodríguez has misplaced his answer key to today's quiz. Help him make a new one. Draw a line from each description to the right picture. Then write the word or words describing each picture to the right. (Careful: there are more pictures than descriptions.)

Despega, vuela y aterriza.
¿Qué es?

el avión _____

Ayuda a los pasajeros. ¿Quién
es?

Ayuda a los viajeros a
comprar billetes. ¿Quién es?

la agente de viajes _____

Muchas personas están en la
entrada. ¿Qué hacen?

descansar _____

¡Hace calor! No quieres hacer
muchas cosas. ¿Qué quieres
hacer?

el equipaje _____

el asistente de vuelo _____

Enrichment: Distribute copies of vocabulary cards for Unidad 1 through Unidad 3 from the Teacher's Resource Book. Students may work in pairs or small groups to create their own quizzes.

hacen fila _____

Nombre _____

D. **What do you answer if you are asked these questions? What do other people answer? Follow the model to answer the questions.**

1. ¿Qué dices si una persona pregunta . . . "¿Quieres ir al cine?"

   Digo que sí. _____

   ¿Qué dices si una persona pregunta . . . "¿Dices mentiras?"

   Digo que sí. *or* Digo que no. _____

   ¿Qué dices si una persona pregunta . . . "¿Te gusta nadar?"

   Digo que sí. *or* Digo que no. _____

2. ¿Qué dice tu maestro si preguntas . . . "¿Puedo abrir la ventana?"

   Dice que sí. *or* Dice que no. _____

   ¿Qué dice tu maestro si preguntas . . . "¿Puedo hablar en voz alta?"

   Dice que sí. *or* Dice que no. _____

   ¿Qué dice tu maestro si preguntas . . . "¿Puedo estar en el patio y no ir a clase?"

   Dice que sí. *or* Dice que no. _____

3. ¿Qué dicen tus papás si preguntas . . . "¿Puedo ir al cine con mis amigos?"

   Dicen que sí. *or* Dicen que no. _____

   ¿Qué dicen tus papás si preguntas . . . "¿Puedo ir al parque?"

   Dicen que sí. *or* Dicen que no. _____

   ¿Qué dicen tus papás si preguntas . . . "¿Podemos ver la tele?"

   Dicen que sí. *or* Dicen que no. _____

Nombre _____

E. What do people around you do? Join words from the two columns. Add activities to write complete sentences below.

Yo   hace
Mi mamá   hacemos
Mi maestro   hacen
Mis amigos   hago
Yo y Sara   haces
Ustedes
Tú

1. Answers will vary. _____

2. _____

3. _____

4. _____

5. _____

6. _____

F. You go to a very international school. Many of your classmates come from other countries. Explain to Carlos, a new student, what nationality everyone is.

M Juan es de Chile. Él es _____ chileno _____.

1. Rosa es de Venezuela. Ella es _____ venezolana _____.

2. Felipe es de Bolivia. Él es _____ boliviano _____.

3. Marta y Eugenia son de México. Ellas son _____ mexicanas _____.

4. Thomas es de los Estados Unidos. Él es _____ estadounidense _____.

5. Manolo y Magda son de España. Ellos son _____ españoles _____.

Nombre _____

G. Isabel is showing you her photo album and telling you about her family. Complete her sentences using the verbs *ser, estar* or *ir* in the correct form.

Mi papá _____ **es** _____ agente de viajes.

Ahora _____ **está** _____ en Argentina.

_____ **Va** _____ en avión a muchos países.

1.

Mi mamá _____ **es** _____ artista.

Ahora _____ **está** _____ en Europa.

_____ **Va** _____ a Europa una vez al año.

2.

Éstas _____ **somos** _____ mi hermana y yo.

_____ **Estamos** _____ en la playa de vacaciones.

Todos los años _____ **vamos** _____ a la playa.

3.

Ellos _____ **son** _____ mis abuelos.

_____ **Están** _____ en su casa, en Puerto Rico.

A veces _____ **van** _____ de viaje.

Nombre _____

H. How can you combine these elements so that they make sense? Write
sentences, matching the different parts, and remember to put the verbs from
the second column in the correct form.

Mi hermana	poder	la ventana de la habitación.
Los viajeros	pensar	la clase de arte a las 12 P.M.
La asistente de vuelo	volver	cerrar la puerta?
El agentes de viajes	cerrar	ir de viaje a Europa.
Yo	probar	de Buenos Aires.
¿Ustedes	comenzar	la computadora nueva.

M ____ **Mi hermana piensa ir de viaje a Europa.** _____

1. _Answers will vary. Accept reasonable answers._ _____

2. _____

3. _____

4. _____

5. _____

¿Cómo se dice?

Nombre _____

Textbook pages 150–153

○ **A.** You are standing in a hallway at your hotel. What can you see? Unscramble the syllables of the words below, and then write the correct number next to the word. Remember to add *el, la, las,* or *los.*

M ta-ha-cio-bi-nes	las habitaciones	4
1. te-ar guo-an-ti	el arte antiguo	2
2. ve-lla	la llave	7
3. as-sor-cen	el ascensor	3
4. ris-tu-ta	el turista	6
	la turista	5
5. te-ar der-mo-no	el arte moderno	1

¿Cómo se dice?

Nombre _____

Textbook pages 154–157

A. Look at these objects. Some are usually found in the bedroom, and some in the bathroom. Write the names of the objects in the correct columns.

El dormitorio	El cuarto de baño
la cama	**la bañera**
la sábana	el jabón
las tarjetas postales	la ducha
la manta	la toalla
el teléfono	el agua fría
	el agua caliente

Extension: Have students add names of other items that may be found in these rooms. Then elicit the adjectives **duro/a, blando/a,** by pointing at objects and asking **¿Cómo es la cama? ¿Cómo es la manta?** etc.

¿Cómo se dice?   Nombre _____

Textbook pages 158–161

A. You are interviewing your friend Raquel about her daily routine when she is on vacation. Complete each of your questions with the right form of the word in parentheses. Then complete Raquel's answer.

M **P:** Raquel, ¿a qué hora _____**te despiertas**_____? (despertarse)

R: _____**Me despierto**_____ a las nueve y media.

1. **P:** ¿Quién _____**se baña**_____ primero, tus hermanos o tú? (bañarse)

R: Yo siempre _____**me baño**_____ primero. Ellos nunca _____**se bañan**_____ por la mañana.

2. **P:** ¿Qué hacen ellos? ¿_____**Se lavan**_____? (lavarse)

R: Sí, siempre_____**se lavan**_____ la cara.

3. **P:** ¿Cuántas veces al día _____**se cepillan**_____ ustedes los dientes? (cepillarse)

R: _____**Nos cepillamos**_____ los dientes cuatro veces al día.

4. **P:** ¿A qué hora _____**se acuestan**_____ ustedes? (acostarse)

R: Mis hermanos _____**se acuestan**_____ a las diez de la noche.

Yo _____**me acuesto**_____ a las once y media.

5. **P:** ¿Quiénes _____**se duermen**_____ primero? (dormirse)

R: Pues, todos nosotros _____**nos dormimos**_____ a la misma hora.

Nombre _____

B. What is the daily routine like in your family when everyone is on vacation? Write four sentences each about what everyone does in the morning and at night.

acostarse   ponerse   quitarse   dormirse

levantarse   despertarse   irse   cepillarse

bañarse   secarse   peinarse   lavarse

Por la mañana

Sentences will vary. Encourage students to use as many reflexive forms as they can.

_____

_____

_____

_____

_____

Por la noche

_____

_____

_____

_____

_____

¿Cómo se dice?

Nombre _____

Textbook pages 162–165

○ **A.** You are checking into a hotel, and find yourself in a long line. The clerk is frantic because everyone is asking him for things. Complete each sentence using the correct form of *pedir*.

M Los turistas de California _____ **piden** _____ más toallas.

1. Una señora y yo _____ **pedimos** _____ jabón.

2. También, yo _____ **pido** _____ unas tarjetas postales.

3. El Sr. Bedoya _____ **pide** _____ dos mantas.

4. Dos niñas y yo _____ **pedimos** _____ almohadas.

5. La Sra. Mora _____ **pide** _____ otra habitación. ¡Sus hijos hablan mucho y ella no puede descansar!

○ **B.** Everyone is talking at once! The hotel clerk cannot hear the requests and is becoming very confused. Help him complete his questions using the correct form of *pedir*.

1. Ustedes _____ **piden** _____ más bañeras, ¿no?

2. Tú _____ **pides** _____ tres sábanas, ¿no?

3. Las mujeres _____ **piden** _____ sillas duras, ¿no?

4. El hombre _____ **pide** _____ tarjetas antiguas, ¿no?

5. La mujer alta _____ **pide** _____ otros hijos, ¿no?

Nombre _____

C. You have made many new acquaintances while on vacation. You want to find someone to play chess with you. Use the correct form of jugar to ask your new friends if they play chess. Then use the pictures to help your friends answer your questions.

el tenis   el dominó   el fútbol americano
el fútbol   el baloncesto   el ajedrez

M Arturo y Víctor, ¿_____**juegan**_____ ustedes al ajedrez?

No, nosotros jugamos al fútbol americano.

1. Carmen, ¿_____**juegas**_____ al ajedrez?

No, yo juego al dominó.

2. Violeta y Dolores, ¿_____**juegan**_____ ustedes al ajedrez?

No, nosotras jugamos al tenis.

3. Francisco, _____**juegas**_____ tú al ajedrez?

No, yo juego al baloncesto.

4. Benito y Celia, ¿_____**juegan**_____ ustedes al ajedrez?

No, nosotros jugamos al fútbol.

5. Armando, ¿_____**juegas**_____ tú al ajedrez?

Sí, yo juego al ajedrez.

¡A leer!

Nombre _____

Read the paragraphs and do the activities below.

Pueblos de encanto

Mazunte es un pueblo muy pequeño del Pacífico, en la costa de México. En Mazunte, el turista puede alquilar una habitación por 10 dólares o dormir por 3 dólares, escuchando el sonido del mar, ¡en una hamaca fuera del hotel!

Cerca de Mazunte, los turistas pueden ver una puesta de sol única. Para llegar a Mazunte, se sale de Oaxaca a Pochutla, pueblo del interior, a 15 kilómetros de distancia de Mazunte.

Luego puedes viajar en **camión** entre los pueblos, no cuesta mucho. Los turistas más atrevidos pueden hacer la ruta caminando, también. Tienen que pensar bien en las cosas más necesarias: mochila con toalla, jabón, abrelatas, refrescos... ¡Qué aventura!

> Nota: **Pueblo** means "town."

Decide which one of these towns is Mazunte, which one is Pochutla, and which one is Oaxaca. Draw the route from Oaxaca to Mazunte as described above.

Complete these sentences.

1. Una habitación en Mazunte cuesta ____diez dólares____.

2. Puedes viajar en ____camión____ o ____a pie (caminando)____.

3. En Mazunte puedo ver una ____puesta del sol____ muy bonita.

4. Si vas a pie, necesitas traer ____mochila con toalla, jabón, abrelatas, refrescos____.

Nombre _____

Conexión con los estudios sociales

In hotels, you can often find signs that tell you what to do and what not to do. Look at these signs and try to match them with their meaning in Spanish.

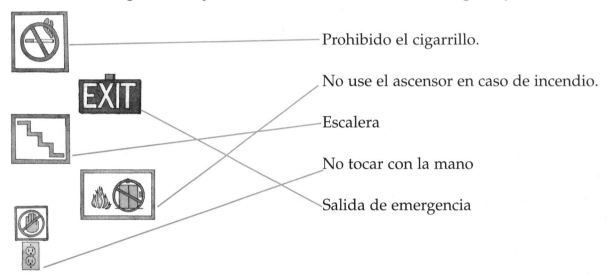

Prohibido el cigarrillo.

No use el ascensor en caso de incendio.

Escalera

No tocar con la mano

Salida de emergencia

Find out about other signs in Spanish, draw them and write what they mean.

Expresa tus ideas

Nombre _____

The Explorers' Club members are attending a conference of master explorers. Club members even get to stay in a hotel! Write at least six sentences about what you see in the picture.

Students' sentences will vary. Possible sentences include: Berta tiene una toalla

muy vieja. Ella pide una toalla nueva. Pepe está cerca del ascensor. Quiere subir.

Luis quiere la llave de la habitación. Está en el pantalón de Pepe. Un hombre sirve

refrescos a Rita y José. Ellos tienen mucha sed. La Srta. Aventura se duerme en un

sillón. Ella tiene todo el equipaje de los alumnos. Ana tiene calor. Se quita el

abrigo. Paco mira a una muchacha bonita. Él la sigue.

_____

_____

_____

_____

 ¡A DIVERTIRSE!

Nombre _____

Un crucigrama

Complete the sentences. Write the missing words in the puzzle.

							¹J	U	E	G	²A		
³T	U	R	I	⁴S	T	⁵A	S				R		
A				E		S		⁶M			T		
R					⁷C	A	L	I	E	⁸N	T	E	
⁹J	A	B	Ó	N		E		S		O			
¹⁰M	E					N		¹¹S	I	G	O		
T						S							
¹²M	A	N	T	A		¹³D	O	R	M	I	M	O	S
S						R							

Horizontales

1. Luis ___ al tenis.

3. Los viajeros a otros países son ___.

7. Siempre me baño con agua ___.

9. Cuando me lavo, uso mucho ___.

10. ___ acuesto temprano.

11. Yo ___ las instrucciones de las actividades.

12. Tienes que poner una ___ en la cama.

13. Primero nos acostamos; luego, nos ___.

Verticales

2. No me gusta mirar el ___ moderno.

3. Rita escribe ___ postales.

4. Hugo ___ despierta a las siete.

5. ¿Puedes subir al techo del hotel en el ___?

6. Son las llaves de mi cuarto. ¡Son ___ llaves!

8. ___ ponemos los abrigos en el invierno.

¿Cómo se dice?

Textbook pages 170–173

Nombre _____

○ **A.** Jorge has earned money by washing cars. What does he do with his money? Look at the pictures, and then write the missing words on the lines provided.

Tengo muchos **M**  y unas **(1)** . Voy al **(2)**  y

busco una **(3)** abierta. ¡Qué bueno! Conozco a una **(4)** .

Es la mamá de mi amigo Paco. Ella dice que Paco está en la

(5) .

M	_____ **billetes** _____	2.	_____ banco _____	4.	_____ cajera _____
1.	_____ monedas _____	3.	_____ ventanilla _____	5.	_____ escuela _____

¡Piénsalo!

Imagine it's 3:30 on Monday right now. Look at the opening hours of these stores and restaurants and write next to them whether they are open or closed right now.

Lunes a viernes, 10:00–2:00 y 5:00–8:00. ____ **cerrado** ____

Todos los días, 7:00–4:00 ____ abierto ____

Fines de semana solamente, 10:00–5:00 ____ cerrado ____

Lunes a viernes, 8:00–5:00, sábados 8:00–12:00 ____ abierto ____

Todos los días, 1:00-10:00, cerrado los lunes ____ cerrado ____

¿Cómo se dice?

Nombre _____

Textbook pages 174–177

○ **A.** You are dining out. What can you see? Write the name of each picture next to the correct number.

   2.    4.

1.    3.    5.

M _____ **el menú** _____   3. _____ **el restaurante** _____

1. _____ **el camarero** _____   4. _____ **la cuenta** _____

2. _____ **la camarera** _____   5. _____ **la propina** _____

○ **B.** Nuria and Luis are sitting right behind you. Can you fill in the missing words in their conversation? Use the words you wrote in A.

NURIA: ¿Te gusta este _____ **restaurante** _____?

LUIS: Sí, mucho. Es muy bonito y muy tranquilo.

NURIA: El _____ **menú** _____ tiene platos muy buenos.

LUIS: Sí, es verdad. Y la _____ **camarera** _____ es muy simpática.

NURIA: Voy a pedir la _____ **cuenta** _____.

LUIS: Está bien. Y yo voy a dejar una buena _____ **propina** _____.

¿Cómo se dice?

Nombre _____

Textbook pages 178–181

A. Martina and Iris went to the petting zoo together. Now Martina is showing Iris the pictures her dad took. Look at the pictures and match them with what Martina is saying.

A

C

E

B

D

1. Le doy sal a la llama. _____ C

2. Aquí te doy una galleta a ti. _____ D

3. Sandra y Rogelio me dan galletas. _____ B

4. Le damos las gracias a mi papá. _____ E

5. Yo le doy un abrazo a mi mamá. _____ A

Nombre _____

B. Paula had neatly written in her computer all the forms of the verb *dar*, but someone has played a joke on her and scrambled all the letters. Can you help her? Unscramble the letters and then use the words to complete the sentences below.

M Yo ydo _____**doy**_____.

Tú ads _____**das**_____.

Él, ella, usted ad _____**da**_____.

Nosotros, nosotras adoms

_____**damos**_____.

Ellos, ellas, ustedes nad

_____**dan**_____.

M Yo le _____**doy**_____ la mano a mi amigo

El camarero nos _____**da**_____ la cuenta.

Nosotros le _____**damos**_____ una propina al camarero.

Tú me _____**das**_____ los libros.

Ustedes siempre nos _____**dan**_____ las gracias.

Los perros nos _____**dan**_____ miedo.

Yo le _____**doy**_____ un abrazo a mi papá.

C. Who ends up doing the shopping in Manuel's family? Look at the pictures and write sentences about what Manuel says using the verb *dar*.

M _____**Mamá me da un billete.**_____

1. _____Yo le doy el billete a mi hermano. (Accept reasonable variations.)_____

2. _____Mi hermano le da el billete al vendedor._____

3. _____Mi hermano me da la leche._____

4. _____Yo le doy la leche a mi mamá._____

¿Cómo se dice?

Nombre _____

Textbook pages 182–185

A. Can you tell the present from the past? Look at these verbs and circle the ones that are not in the past.

gasté	cambiaste	(gastan)
ahorramos	(cambias)	ahorraron
(ahorro)	gastaste	cambió

You may wish to point out that the **nosotros** form of these verbs is the same in the present and in the past (**ahorramos, cambiamos,** etc.)

B. Use the above verbs in the correct form to complete these sentences:

M Ayer Javier _____ **cambió** _____ los pantalones en la tienda.

1. ¿_____ **Gastaste** _____ todo el dinero en libros?

2. ¿_____ **Cambiaste** _____ los dólares por pesos en el banco?

3. _____ **Ahorramos** _____ casi $10 comprando en las rebajas.

4. No _____ **gasté** _____ todo el dinero. Tengo casi $50.

5. Mis papás _____ **ahorraron** _____ dinero durante el año y ahora nos vamos de vacaciones.

Nombre _____

C. What did you and your friends do last week? Complete the sentences with the verbs from the box in the correct form.

| comprar | bailar | ayudar | caminar | limpiar | estudiar |

M La semana pasada nosotros _____ **compramos** _____ unos pantalones y unas botas.

1. Ayer yo _____ limpié _____ mi habitación.

2. El año pasado mi familia y yo _____ ahorramos _____ mucho dinero.

3. La semana pasada _____ ayudé _____ a mi hermano con las tareas.

4. Ayer Paco _____ estudió _____ la lección de estudios sociales.

5. Sara y su hermana _____ bailaron _____ mucho en la fiesta.

6. ¿_____ Caminaron _____ mucho ustedes ayer?

D. This is Berta's diary. Here she writes everything she does in the week. Since her Spanish is getting good, she started writing it in Spanish. But today she is having trouble with her verbs. Help her! Write the correct verb in the correct form.

Querido diario:

Hoy es domingo y tengo mucho sueño. La semana pasada estudié mucho. El sábado

_____ **compré** _____ un disco compacto y _____ gasté _____ todo mi dinero

ahorrado. Pero me gusta mucho, así que estoy muy feliz. El sábado mamá también me

_____ compró _____ unas pinturas y un cuaderno para dibujar. Por la tarde papá y

yo _____ limpiamos _____ el garaje. David _____ ayudó _____ a mamá en la cocina

y ellos dos _____ cocinaron _____ una torta muy buena. Hoy_____ caminamos _____

todos por la montaña y por la tarde _____ descansamos _____.

¡A leer!

Nombre _____

Read the following text and answer the questions.

Los bancos

La palabra «banco» tiene diferentes significados. Un banco es el lugar donde te sientas en una plaza o un parque. También, «banco» es en algunos países sinónimo de «pupitre». En algunos países, la mesa de trabajo de la cocina se llama «banco» también. Finalmente, un «banco» es un lugar donde las personas dejan su dinero para tenerlo bien guardado.

Make a drawing for each of the meanings of the word «banco».

Nombre _____

Conexión con las matemáticas

You've taken a trip around South America and have brought souvenirs for your friends and family. You remember the prices in dollars of everything. Now you want to remember what the actual prices were in local currencies. Use the exchange rates below to make the calculations. Then, write down a description of what you bought.

Nota: A *wallet* is called **una cartera.**

$5 = _____**17.5**_____ nuevos soles

Compré un sombrero peruano. _____

$4 = _____**30.8**_____ bolivianos

Compré unas carteras bolivianas. _____

$23 = _____**14,191**_____ pesos chilenos

Compré un sombrero chileno. _____

$35 = _____**101.5**_____ pesos argentinos

Compré un poncho argentino. _____

Exchange Rates
$1 = 2.9 pesos argentinos $1 = 3.5 nuevos soles (peruanos)
$1 = 7.7 bolivianos $1 = 617 pesos chilenos

⚙ ¡APRENDE MÁS! ⚙

Nombre _____

In this unit you have learned two expressions with the verb **dar: dar las gracias** and **dar la mano.** This small but useful verb is part of many expressions.

Read the following conversations and study the pictures. The expression with the verb *dar* is in heavy black letters. On the line below the picture and the conversation, write what you think the expression means.

1. JORGE: Iris, ¿cuál te gusta más: el gato grande o el gato pequeño?

    IRIS: **Me da lo mismo.** Me gusta el grande y me gusta el pequeño.

It's the same to me. Wording may vary.

2. TONY: Este vendedor siempre llega a las dos para vender sus aspiradoras.

    ANITA: ¿Qué haces?

    TONY: **¡Le doy con la puerta en las narices!**

"I shut the door in his face!"

3. MAMÁ: Mi hijo siempre estudia. Lee sus libros a todas horas. **No se da cuenta de que** hay otras personas en la casa.

    AMIGA: ¿Por qué no le escribes una carta?

He doesn't realize or notice.

You may wish to write the expressions on the chalkboard in their infinitive forms: (1) **dar lo mismo** (or **dar igual**), "to be all the same"; (2) **darle con la puerta en las narices,** "to shut the door in someone's face"; (3) **darse cuenta de que,** "to realize, to notice."

Extension: Have students find other expressions with dar in a Spanish-English dictionary (for example, **darse por vencido; dar de comer; dar en el clavo; darse aires**).

¡A DIVERTIRSE! Nombre _____

El juego del treinta y cuatro

Unscramble the word and write it on the line. Then, find the number of the word in the lists below and write the number in the circle. The sum of each row, across or down, should equal 34. The first word has been done for you.

vancteo (4) centavo	seops (5) pesos	aifl (9) fila	acroder (16) cerrado	34
acejra (2) cajera	atecus (10) cuesta	llaitnevna (8) ventanilla	asopagm (14) pagamos	34
unceta (13) cuenta	ronpipa (7) propina	tragsa (11) gastar	ledsaró (3) dólares	34
botarie (15) abierto	rhoarra (12) ahorrar	nesdoma (6) monedas	nobca (1) banco	34

1. el banco
2. la cajera
3. los dólares
4. el centavo
5. los pesos
6. las monedas
7. la propina
8. la ventanilla
9. hacer fila
10. cuesta
11. gastar
12. ahorrar
13. la cuenta
14. pagamos
15. abierto
16. cerrado

¿Cómo se dice?   Nombre _____

Textbook pages 190–193

○ **A.** **Who is who? Read the sentences, look at the picture and write the names of the people.**

Tell students to use their own left and right as reference.

Pablo está muy cerca de la fuente.

Erica está delante del museo.

Marcos está a la derecha de la alcaldía.

Guillermo está detrás de la escultura.

Santi está a la izquierda del monumento.

Lola está a la derecha del monumento.

Where is everyone?

_____En la plaza._____

◑ **B.** **Write one more sentence about each of the children in A, using *cerca de* and *lejos de.***

M _____ **Pablo está lejos del museo.** _____

1. _Answers will vary._____

2. _____

3. _____

4. _____

5. _____

6. _____

¿Cómo se dice?

Nombre _____

A. Your friends have many errands to run today. They are asking for your advice. Use the list to answer their questions.

el zoológico   ✓ la alcaldía   el museo

el metro   el supermercado

M EDUARDO: Tengo que ir a las oficinas de la ciudad. Tengo que recoger unos papeles importantes. ¿Adónde voy?

TÚ: Tienes que ir _____**a la alcaldía**_____.

1. MARÍA: Mi mamá necesita arroz, carne, pan y tortillas. Yo tengo que comprar todo. ¿Adónde voy?

TÚ: Tienes que ir _____al supermercado_____.

2. RUDY: Para la clase de ciencias, tengo que sacar fotos de tigres, osos y leones. ¿Dónde puedo sacar las fotos?

TÚ: Tienes que ir _____al zoológico_____.

3. LUPE: Tengo que escribir un reporte sobre el arte antiguo. ¿Adónde voy para ver el arte antiguo?

TÚ: Tienes que ir _____al museo (de arte)_____.

4. DAVID: Tengo que ir a otra parte de la ciudad. No hay autobús. ¿Cómo voy?

TÚ: Tienes que tomar _____el metro_____.

¿Cómo se dice?   Nombre _____

Textbook pages 198–202

A. The Novas family is at home. It is 6 P.M. and everyone is busy. Read the sentences and label each family member. Once you have identified everyone, write a sentence about what each is doing.

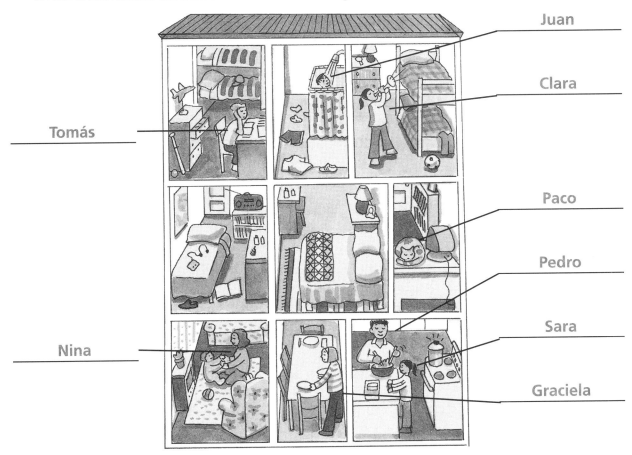

Juan

Clara

Tomás

Paco

Pedro

Sara

Nina

Graciela

M Nina y el bebé están en la sala de estar. ___ **Están jugando.** ___

1. Tomás está en su dormitorio.

   ___ **Está estudiando.** ___

2. Clara está en su dormitorio.

   ___ **Está tocando la trompeta.** ___

3. Graciela no está en su dormitorio.

   ___ **Está poniendo la mesa.** ___

4. Paco está en el despacho.

   ___ **Está durmiendo.** ___

5. Juan está en el baño.

   ___ **Se está duchando.** ___

6. Pedro y Sara están en la cocina.

   ___ **Están cocinando.** ___

Nombre _____

B. What do you think these people feel like? Describe how they feel using the words in the box (remember to use the correct form).

contento	cansado	enojado	triste	confundido	nervioso

M Paula trabaja diez horas al día y duerme muy poco.

Está cansada.

1. Tenemos un examen esta mañana y no estudiamos mucho ayer.

   Estamos nerviosos *or* nerviosas.

2. Sandra tiene vacaciones y se va de viaje.

   Está contenta.

3. Miguel no puede ir de excursión porque está enfermo.

   Está triste.

4. Tu hermano no ayuda en casa y tú tienes que hacer todo.

   Estoy enojado *or* enojada.

5. El camarero dice que no tenemos que pagar la cena. No sabemos por qué.

   Estamos confundidos *or* confundidas.

C. How is the clown feeling? Look at the picture and say how you think he is feeling. You can use more than one adjective.

Answers will vary.

_____

_____

Extension: Have students compare their answers in pairs.

¿Cómo se dice?

Nombre _____

Textbook pages 203–207

A. Sr. González had the worst day yesterday. Look at the pictures and number the sentences in order.

1.

4.

2.

5.

3.

6.

M No llegó al autobús a tiempo. ___3___

Salió de casa a las nueve de la mañana. ___1___

Volvió a casa a recoger el paraguas. ___2___

Cayó en la calle. ___5___

Le dolió la mano todo el día. ___6___

Corrió por la calle para llegar a tiempo al trabajo. ___4___

Nombre _____

B. You and your brothers are on vacation at your aunt's home in Madrid. You have been enjoying yourselves, doing a million things. Now your aunt is asking you what you and your brothers have been up to. Complete your answers.

M ¿Cuántas millas corriste ayer? _____ **Corrí** _____ tres millas.

1. ¿Volviste a casa muy tarde? No, _____ **volví** _____ a las siete de la tarde.

2. ¿Tus hermanos salieron ayer por la tarde? No, no _____ **salieron** _____.

3. ¿Volvieron al hotel por la noche? Sí, _____ **volvieron** _____ al hotel a las diez.

4. ¿Saliste con tus amigos la semana pasada? Sí, _____ **salimos** _____ todos juntos.

5. ¿Tu hermano corrió para llegar al tren? No, no _____ **corrió** _____ porque llegó en taxi.

C. Complete these sentences with the correct form of the verbs *correr, salir, volver,* or *doler.*

M Ayer mis hermanos y yo _____ **corrimos dos millas por el parque** _____.

1. ¿La semana pasada tú _____ **Answers will vary.** _____?

2. Ayer por la noche Antonio y Elena _____.

3. En Nueva York nosotras _____.

4. Tú y tú hermano no _____.

5. Ayer ustedes _____.

6. Ayer la pierna me _____.

¡A leer!

Nombre _____

Read the following text and decide whether the statements are true or false. Rewrite any false statements so that they are true.

En México DF

En México DF, dentro de la ciudad, hay una buena red de metro y muchos «peseros». Los peseros son camionetas o pequeños camiones que, por dos pesos, te llevan como un autobús. Para comer, un buen destino es el restaurante El Bajío.

Cerca de la plaza mayor, o zócalo, está la Secretaría de Educación Pública, que tiene murales de Diego Rivera dentro de un doble patio. Los viajeros visitan el Museo de Antropología o el Templo Mayor.

Si quieres ir de excursión, dicen que visitar las pirámides de Teotihuacán, a menos de una hora de distancia, es fantástico. Taxco, una ciudad colonial a más de dos horas de distancia de México DF, es muy bonita.

1. En la capital de México no hay metro.

Falso. En México DF hay una buena red de metro. _____

2. Los «peseros» son coches pequeños.

Falso. Son autobuses para todas las personas. _____

3. En México, las plazas también se llaman zócalos.

Cierto. _____

4. En la capital de México hay casas con patios.

Cierto. _____

5. En Taxco hay unas pirámides fantásticas.

Falso. En Teotihuacán hay unas pirámides fantásticas. _____

6. Taxco es una bonita ciudad colonial mexicana.

Cierto. _____

Nombre _____

Conexión con los estudios sociales

In Spanish-speaking countries there are still small stores that, unlike supermarkets, specialize in one type of product (food or others). Many stores have names that come from the object they sell. Can you guess what these stores sell? Write sentences saying what you bought at each store yesterday.

la pescadería: **Ayer en la pescadería compramos pescado.** _____

la panadería: Ayer en la panadería compramos pan. _____

la mueblería: Ayer en la mueblería compramos muebles. _____

la verdulería: Ayer en la verdulería compramos verduras. _____

la carnicería: Ayer en la carnicería compramos carne. _____

la zapatería: Ayer en la zapatería compramos zapatos. _____

la frutería: Ayer en la frutería compramos fruta. _____

Point out that **la zapatería** can also be a place where shoes are fixed, not sold.

Nombre _____

Expresa tus ideas

The Explorers' Club is at the bus station, waiting for the bus to Villahermosa. Each of the members decides to wait doing something different. Look at the picture and write at least seven sentences that describe what they are doing and how they are feeling.

Students' sentences will vary. Possible sentences include: La Srta. Aventura está

mirando un mapa. La Srta. Aventura está contenta. Pepe y Rita están durmiendo.

Ana y Luis están jugando a cartas. Ana y Luis están enojados. José está comiendo

un sándwich y bebiendo un jugo. José está triste. Paco está mirando el horario.

Paco está confundido. Berta está cansada.

¡A DIVERTIRSE!

Nombre _____

Busca las diferencias

Ciudad Hermosa is a big city. It even has two big plazas—Plaza Central and Plaza Colón. Write several sentences about the differences between the two plazas.

Sentences will vary.

_____

_____

_____

_____

_____

_____

Nombre _____

A. Whenever you go anywhere with your little sister Hortensia, she always has lots of questions. Write an answer to each question based on what you see in the picture.

M P: ¿Qué te da la cajera?

R: _____**Ella me da unas monedas.**_____

1. P: ¿Qué le dan los hombres al cajero?

R: _____*Ellos le dan unos billetes.*_____

2. P: ¿Qué nos da primero el camarero?

R: _____*Primero, (él) nos da el menú. OR Nos da el menú primero.*_____

3. P: Después de comer, ¿qué le das al camarero?

R: _____*Yo le doy una propina (después de comer).*_____

4. P: Antes de irnos, ¿qué nos da la camarera?

R: _____*Ella nos da la cuenta.*_____

Nombre _____

B. You and your family just won a week's vacation at Hotel Buen Descanso. What will you do while you're there? Complete each sentence with the correct form of the word in parentheses.

M Todos _____pedimos_____ una almohada blanda. (pedir)

1. Mi hermano y yo _____queremos_____ jugar al volibol en la playa. (querer)

2. Yo _____almuerzo_____ temprano cada mañana. (almorzar)

3. Mis padres _____piden_____ unas toallas y unas sábanas. (pedir)

4. Mis hermanos y yo _____jugamos_____ al tenis dos días a la semana. (jugar)

5. Hace fresco por la noche. Todos _____pedimos_____ unas mantas. (pedir)

C. Your new classmate loves asking questions! And you love talking about yourself, so always you answer all of them. Write your answers to his questions.

M ¿Qué pides siempre en el restaurante? _____Pido espaguetis._____

1. ¿A qué juegas en verano con tus amigos? _____Juego a/Jugamos a . . . Answers will vary._____

2. ¿A qué hora almuerzas? _____Almuerzo a . . ._____

3. ¿Qué quieres hacer el día de tu cumpleaños? _____Quiero . . ._____

4. ¿Dónde almuerzan en tu casa? _____Almorzamos en/Almuerzan en . . ._____

Nombre _____

D. This is what Carlos does every morning. Does the order in which he does these things seem alright to you? How would you do them? Number them in the order you would do these things.

Answers may vary. Accept reasonable answers. Sample answers are:

M Se despierta a las siete de la mañana. ___1___

1. Se cepilla el pelo. ___6___

2. Se ducha. ___3___

3. Se quita el pijama. ___2___

4. Se seca el pelo. ___5___

5. Se cepilla los dientes. ___7___

6. Se pone la ropa. ___4___

E. What do you do every night before you go to sleep? Describe you routine before going to bed. Try to write at least five sentences.

M **Me quito la ropa.** _____

1. _Answers will vary._ _____

2. _____

3. _____

4. _____

5. _____

Nombre _____

F. **What did you do yesterday? And last week? What did your friends and family do? Join words from the different columns to make sentences. Put the verbs in the correct forms.**

ayer	limpiar
la semana pasada	gastar
yo	ahorrar
mi hermano	bailar
mis papás	comprar
mi maestro	estudiar
mis amigos	caminar
	descansar

M **Ayer mi hermano estudió mucho.** _____

1. Answers will vary. _____

2. _____

3. _____

4. _____

5. _____

6. _____

Nombre _____

G. **Your friend Marita wants to be a detective when she grows up. She thinks she should start practicing now, and you are helping her with her questions. Write your answers to her questions.**

M ¿A qué hora saliste ayer de casa?

Ayer salí a las 9:20 A.M.

1. ¿A qué hora volviste?

Answers will vary.

2. ¿A qué hora salieron tus hermanos de casa ayer?

_____

3. ¿A qué hora volvieron?

_____

4. ¿A qué hora tu papá o tu mamá volvió a casa?

_____

5. ¿Cuándo corriste por el parque?

_____

6. La semana pasada, ¿volviste algún día tarde con tus hermanos?

_____

7. ¿Te perdiste alguna vez en una ciudad?

_____

8. ¿Te dolió algo la última vez que jugaste a fútbol?

_____

Extension: Have students ask each other the questions and give their answers.

Nombre _____

H. Imagine that you're entering a short-story contest sponsored by the Jardín Zoológico. The winner gets to feed the lions for a week! Look at the picture and write a story with at least five sentences about Sara, Juan, and Raúl. If you need to, use the questions to get started.

_____

_____

_____

_____

_____

_____

Sentences will vary. Encourage students to create their own stories. Possible sentences may include: Sara y Juan están descansando. Raúl está mirando los osos.

¿Dónde están los tres amigos?   ¿Cómo están Sara y Juan?

¿Están caminando o descansando?   ¿Dónde está la fuente?

¿Cómo está Raúl? ¿Está nervioso?   ¿Qué está mirando Raúl?

Extension: To practice commands, have students create a conversation among the three friends:
Raúl: ¡Mira, Sara! Hay dos osos. ¡Qué tristes están!
Sara: Estoy cansada. Descansa, Raúl.
Juan: Sí, descansa. ¡No camines más!

¿Cómo se dice?

Nombre _____

Textbook pages 212–215

○ **A.** Your friend Rogelio has lost Sultán, his dog. You and two other friends have offered to help search for the dog. Rogelio has drawn a map for you to follow. Complete the sentences based on the map.

```
--------- Felipe
-·-·-·- Carmen
············· Yo
```

X   N

O   E

S

M Comenzamos en ____ **la esquina** ____.

1. Comenzamos cerca ____ **del farol** ____.

2. Felipe va a caminar ____ **una cuadra** ____ al este.

3. Carmen va a caminar una cuadra ____ **al este** ____ también.

Luego, va a doblar a la derecha y caminar ____ **al sur** ____.

Por último, ella va a doblar a la derecha y caminar ____ **al oeste** ____.

4. Yo voy a caminar por las dos ____ **manzanas** ____.

5. En quince minutos, volvemos a la X en ____ **la esquina** ____.

¿Cómo se dice?

Nombre _____

Textbook pages 216–219

A. You are taking your little sister for a walk. How do you answer her questions? Use the pictures.

M ¿Cómo va el autobús?

El autobús va despacio.

1. ¿Dónde queda el restaurante?

El restaurante queda más atrás.

2. ¿Por qué ese niño mira un mapa?

Porque no quiere perderse.

3. ¿Cómo van los coches?

Los coches van rápido.

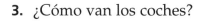

4. ¿Por dónde tenemos que caminar ahora?

Tenemos que caminar por el paso de peatones.

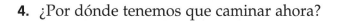

5. ¿Dónde queda el cine?

El cine queda más adelante.

6. ¿Con quién vamos a encontrarnos?

Vamos a encontrarnos con mamá.

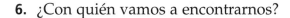

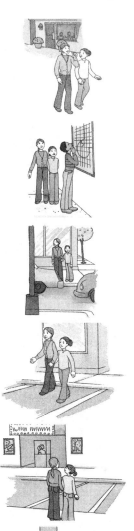
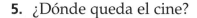

¿Cómo se dice?   Nombre _____

Textbook pages 220–224

A. Some people, like Lucía, are naturally bossy. When she gets home, her younger brothers and sisters get the benefit of her natural bossy talents! Complete the commands.

M CARLOTA: ¡No me cepillo los dientes!

    LUCÍA: Carlota, _____ **¡cepíllate los dientes!** _____

1. DANIEL: ¡No me quito los zapatos!

    LUCÍA: Daniel, _____ **¡quítate los zapatos!** _____

2. JULIA: ¡No leo el libro!

    LUCÍA: Julia, _____ **¡lee el libro!** _____

3. PABLO: ¡No me lavo las manos!

    LUCÍA: Pablo, _____ **¡lávate las manos!** _____

4. MATEO: ¡No abro la puerta!

    LUCÍA: Mateo, _____ **¡abre la puerta!** _____

5. GLORIA: ¡No me baño!

    LUCÍA: Gloria, _____ **¡báñate!** _____

6. INÉS: ¡No me lavo y no me seco la cara!

    LUCÍA: Inés, _____ **¡lávate y sécate la cara!** _____

6. SANDRA: ¡No corro a la cama!

    LUCÍA: Sandra, _____ **¡corre a la cama!** _____

7. CARLOS: No me peino. ¡No me cepillo los dientes tampoco!

    LUCÍA: Carlos, _____ **¡péinate! ¡Y cepíllate los dientes (también)!** _____

8. PILAR: ¡No estudio las matemáticas!

    LUCÍA: Pilar, _____ **¡estudia las matemáticas!** _____

Nombre _____

B. Imagine that you write an advice column. You have received the following letters. What advice do you give the letter writers? Tell the writers what to do, and what not to do.

¡Hola!

A mí me gusta el frío. A mi hermano le gusta el calor. Yo siempre abro la ventana pero él la cierra. ¿Qué hago?

Alma Ventana

Answers will vary.
_____
_____
_____
_____

¡Hola!

Tengo que leer dos libros este fin de semana. No quiero leerlos. Quiero ir al cine con mis amigos. También quiero ir al museo y jugar al fútbol. ¿Qué hago?

Pedro Juegamucho

_____
_____
_____
_____
_____

¡Hola!

A mí me gusta llevar mi chaqueta favorita siempre. Siempre tengo buena suerte cuando llevo mi chaqueta. Mi mamá me dice: "¡Quítate la chaqueta en la casa! ¡No vivimos en un estadio!" ¿Qué hago?

Juan Llévalo

_____
_____
_____
_____
_____

¿Cómo se dice?

Nombre _____

Textbook pages 225–229

○ **A.** Would you like to know what Pablo did last week? Join the two columns and find out.

M El lunes llegué   en la casa de mi abuela Emma.

1. El martes pagué   al fútbol con mi amigo Juan.

2. El miércoles saqué   tarde a la clase de ciencias.

3. El jueves almorcé   el almuerzo de mi amigo Andrés.

4. El viernes comencé   al perro por la mañana y por la noche.

5. El sábado jugué   una nueva clase.

6. El domingo sequé   mi ropa en el jardín.

● **B.** Now that you know what Pablo did, tell your friend Florencia about it (remember to change the verbs and other words that you need to change!)

M El lunes llegó tarde a la clase de ciencias.

1. El martes pagó el almuerzo de su amigo Andrés.

2. El miércoles sacó al perro por la mañana y por la noche.

3. El jueves almorzó en la casa de su abuela Emma.

4. El viernes comenzó una nueva clase.

5. El sábado jugó al fútbol con su amigo Juan.

6. El domingo secó su ropa en el jardín.

Nombre _____

C. What did Pablo's friends do last week? Complete the sentences with the verbs in the correct form and you will know.

M Carolina: Yo _____**almorcé**_____ (almorzar) con Ricardo en un restaurante.

1. Tomás: Yo _____**jugué**_____ (jugar) en el parque.

2. Elvira: Yo _____**saqué**_____ (sacar) la ropa vieja de mi dormitorio.

3. Ricardo: Yo _____**comencé**_____ (comenzar) un libro nuevo.

4. Anita: Yo _____**llegué**_____ (llegar) temprano a clase todos los días.

D. What did you do last week? Answer the questions.

M ¿A qué hora llegaste a casa ayer?

Llegué a casa a las siete de la tarde. _____

2. ¿Compraste algo en la tienda? ¿Cuánto pagaste?

Answers will vary. _____

3. ¿Qué días sacaste la basura?

_____

4. ¿Con quién almorzaste el sábado?

_____

5. ¿Dónde jugaste el viernes?

_____

Extension: Have students compare their answers in pairs.

¡A leer!

Nombre _____

Read the following message and answer the questions.

email message from icarregal@planeta.com to amoreno@caribe.com

Querida Anita:

Como vas a viajar a Colombia la próxima semana, hablé por teléfono con mi prima Elvira. Ella vive en Cali. No pierdas la oportunidad: visita a su familia. Habla con ella.

En Cali siempre hace buen tiempo y hay mucha música. Dicen que es la capital "salsera" de Colombia.

Para llegar a Cali desde Bogotá, toma el avión a Santiago de Cali. En el aeropuerto, toma un taxi. Los taxis son muy baratos y circulan muy rápido por toda la ciudad las 24 horas.

La casa de Elvira y su familia queda en el centro, cerca de la plaza de Caicedo, detrás de unos edificios de apartamentos. Marqué su casa con una cruz en el mapa. Mira el mapa para que puedas llegar fácilmente.

Inés

1. ¿Quién va a viajar a Colombia?

   Anita va a viajar a Colombia.

2. ¿Con quién habló Inés por teléfono?

   Inés habló con su prima Elvira por teléfono.

3. ¿Hace mucho frío en Cali?

   No, siempre hace buen tiempo en Cali.

4. ¿Cuesta mucho viajar en taxi en Cali?

   No, viajar en taxi es muy barato en Cali.

5. ¿Dónde queda la casa de Elvira y su familia? Queda en el centro, cerca de la

   plaza de Caicedo, detrás de unos edificios de apartamentos.

Write three things that Inés tells Anita to do.

_____

_____

Nombre _____

Conexión con los estudios sociales

Look at these events in history and their dates. Then, write a paragraph telling when all these events happened, placing them in order (use the past tense!).

1492 Cristóbal Colón llega a América.

1620 Los peregrinos *(Pilgrims)* llegan a América.

1776 Comienza la Guerra de Independencia estadounidense.

1803 Estados Unidos paga quince millones de dólares por la Compra de Louisiana.

1861 Comienza la Guerra *(War)* Civil estadounidense.

1869 El primer tren llega de Nueva York a San Francisco.

1965 Comienza la Guerra de Vietnam.

1871 El equipo de Cleveland y el de Fort Wayne (Indiana) juega el primer partido profesional de béisbol.

1626 Los holandeses *(The Dutch)* pagan a los indígenas nativos 25 dólares por la isla de Manhattan.

Cristobal Colón llegó a América en 1492.

Answers may vary. Sample paragraph: Los peregrinos llegaron a América en 1620.

Los holandeses pagaron a los indígenas nativos 25 dólares por la isla de

Manhattan en 1626. En 1776 comenzó la Guerra de la Independencia

estadounidense. Estados Unidos pagó quince millones de dólares por la Compra

de Louisiana en 1803. En 1861 comenzó la Guerra Civil estadounidense. El primer

tren llegó de Nueva York a San Francisco en 1869. El equipo de Cleveland y el

equipo de Fort Wayne (Indiana) jugaron el primer partido profesional de béisbol

en 1871. En 1965 comenzó la Guerra de Vietnam.

¡APRENDE MÁS!

Nombre _____

Synonyms are words that have similar meanings. *Antonyms* are words that have opposite meanings. Nouns, verbs, adjectives, and prepositions can have antonyms. You already know many **antónimos,** such as the following:

día—noche   subir—bajar   blanco—negro   delante—detrás
menos—más   caminar—correr   grande—pequeño   cerca—lejos

In the lists below are words you know. For some, you already know the antonym. For others, you may have to find the antonym in a Spanish-English dictionary. The first one has been done for you.

Palabra

1. ahorrar   **gastar**

2. rápido   despacio

3. acostarse   levantarse

4. fuerte   débil

5. debajo de   sobre

6. escribir   borrar*

7. buscar   encontrar

8. generoso   tacaño*

9. cómico   serio*

10. lavarse   secarse

11. limpio   sucio

12. con   sin*

13. hablar   callar

14. izquierda   derecha

15. ponerse   quitarse

The asterisk (*) in the answers indicates vocabulary the students have not learned. You may wish to give them clues to find these words in a Spanish-English dictionary.

¡A DIVERTIRSE!

Nombre _____

Un juego de modismos

How sharp are your detective skills? On this page there are five expressions and illustrations. First, read the sentences with the expressions. (The expressions, or *modismos,* are in heavy black type.) Then look at the pictures. When you think an expression matches a picture, write the number of the sentence in the blank to the right of the picture.

1. **A lo lejos,** podemos ver las montañas.

   3

2. **¡Cuidado con** el tráfico!

   4

3. Paula va a llegar **dentro de poco.**

   2

4. Les **hace falta** la práctica.

   5

5. **Tengo ganas** de comer un helado.

   1

¿Cómo se dice?

Nombre _____

Textbook pages 234–237

○ **A.** These two people work at a jewelry store. What are they wearing? What are they carrying? Write an X in the correct column.

	la joyera	el joyero
unas joyas	X	X
un regalo		X
un brazalete	X	
un llavero		X
un collar	X	
un anillo		X
unos aretes	X	

¿Cómo se dice?

Textbook pages 238–241

Nombre _____

A. Look at these items. Do you find them expensive or inexpensive? Write the name in the correct column, according to what you think.

Answers will vary. The following items must be present: **el audiocasete, el cinturón, el disco compacto, la bolsa, las sandalias, los zapatos.**

barato	caro

Now write sentences about the items you placed in each column.

El audiocasete es muy caro.

_____

_____

_____

_____

_____

¿Cómo se dice?

Nombre _____

Textbook pages 242–245

A. Can you match these questions with their answers?

Preguntas:

Respuestas:

M ¿Qué hiciste ayer por la tarde? ————— Estudié en la biblioteca.

1. ¿Qué hizo Patricia el sábado por la mañana?

   Hizo mucho sol, pero un poco de frío.

2. ¿Fuiste al parque con tus padres ayer?

   Fueron fantásticas.

3. ¿Qué tal las vacaciones?

   Fuimos a un restaurante colombiano excelente.

4. ¿Qué tiempo hizo?

   Nadó en la piscina.

5. ¿Adónde fueron ustedes ayer?

   Sí, y jugamos con la pelota.

Extension: Encourage students to come up with new answers to the questions.

B. What did Walter and his friends do yesterday? Complete the sentences with the correct form of these verbs to find out.

Ayer mis amigos y yo _____**fuimos**_____ (ir) a casa de Pedro para celebrar su

cumpleaños. _____**Hizo**_____ (hacer) mucho sol y _____**salimos**_____ (salir)

al jardín. Su mamá _____**hizo**_____ (hacer) un pastel de chocolate muy bueno.

La fiesta _____**fue**_____ (ser) muy divertida.

C. Write appropriate questions for these answers.

Answers may vary. Possible answers are provided.

M **¿Adónde fueron Juan y tú esta mañana?**

¿Esta mañana? Juan fue a la clase de español y yo fui a la clase de inglés.

1. **¿Qué hiciste ayer?** *or* **¿Dónde almorzaste ayer?**

Ayer almorcé en casa de mi abuela.

2. **¿Cómo fue la clase de música?**

¡Fue fantástica! Aprendimos a tocar una canción en el piano.

3. **¿Qué tiempo hizo el fin de semana?**

El sábado hizo mal tiempo, pero el domingo hizo mucho sol.

¿Cómo se dice?

Nombre _____

Textbook pages 246–249

A. Match the following causes with their consequences.

M Llovió y la temperatura fue muy baja.

Tuve calor.

Tuve frío.

1. Estudié cinco horas en la biblioteca.

2. Miré una película de miedo.

Estuve cansado.

3. Hizo 110 grados Fahrenheit.

Tuve miedo.

4. Llegué tarde a la fiesta y el helado se terminó.

Tuve dolor.

5. Salí tarde de casa.

Tuve prisa.

6. Estuve en el dentista.

Estuve triste.

Nombre _____

B. A park statue has been stolen! Detective Jiménez is interviewing people from the community to try and find some suspects. He is now interviewing Sr. Ramos about his family's whereabouts. Complete his statements with the correct past-tense form of *estar* or *tener*.

M —¿Dónde _____estuvo_____ su mujer el sábado 16 a las 12 de la mañana?

_____Estuvo_____ descansando en el jardín porque _____tuvo_____ un dolor de cabeza fuerte.

1. —¿Dónde _____estuvieron_____ usted y su hijo?

—_____Estuvimos_____ en la casa. Mi hijo _____tuvo_____ sueño y _____estuvo_____ en la cama toda la tarde. Y yo _____tuve_____ hambre y _____estuve_____ en la cocina.

2. —¿Dónde _____estuvieron_____ los abuelos el sábado?

—_____Estuvieron_____ en el gimnasio. Siempre van al gimnasio los sábados por la mañana.

3. —¿Dónde _____estuvo_____ su hermana el sábado a las doce?

—Mi hermana _____tuvo_____ hambre y _____estuvo_____ en un restaurante.

¡A leer!

Nombre _____

Read the following paragraph and answer the questions.

El museo del espacio

Ayer fui de excursión a un museo del espacio. La profesora de ciencias, que es muy simpática, fue con nosotros. Vimos la reproducción exacta de un cohete que fue a la Luna, varios documentales un poco aburridos, y un pedazo de meteorito. Nos lo pasamos muy bien, ¡fue un gran día!

Pero en el viaje de vuelta, se pinchó la rueda del autobús. Tuvimos que esperar dos horas hasta que el chofer cambió la rueda. ¡Fue muy aburrido! No hicimos nada durante todo ese tiempo. No comimos ni pudimos jugar. Luego encontramos mucho tráfico cuando volvimos. Llegamos muy tarde a la ciudad.

Nuestros padres al vernos llegar pensaron: "¡Qué excursión tan larga! ¡Seguramente se divirtieron mucho!"

Draw a comic strip that shows what happened in the story. Use bubbles to write what people said in each scene.

Drawings will vary. Check for coherence with the text.

Nombre _____

Conexión con los estudios sociales

Look at these names and facts of important people in history. Match the people with who they were and what they did. Write sentences with these facts.

	¿Quién fue?	¿Qué hizo?
Cristóbal Colón	presidente de Estados Unidos	defender los derechos (*rights*) de las mujeres
Sitting Bull	una mujer fuerte	escribir la Declaración de la Independencia
Sacajawea	un marinero de Génova	vencer (*defeat*) al general Custer
Thomas Jefferson	un inventor	llegar a América en 1492
Thomas Edison	un indio nativoamericano	inventar la bombilla eléctrica
Susan B. Anthony	una india nativoamericana	ir con la expedición de Lewis y Clark

Cristóbal Colón fue un marinero de Génova. Llegó a América en 1492.

Sitting Bull fue un indio nativoamericano. Venció al general Custer.

Sacajawea fue una india nativoamericana. Fue con la expedición de Lewis y Clark.

Thomas Jefferson fue presidente de Estados Unidos. Escribió la Declaración de la

Independencia. Thomas Edison fue inventor. Inventó la bombilla eléctrica.

Susan B. Anthony fue una mujer fuerte. Defendió los derechos de las mujeres.

_____

_____

_____

Expresa tus ideas   Nombre _____

Señorita Aventura's birthday is tomorrow. The Explorers' Club members are
meeting at Rita's house to show off the gifts they bought. What is their
conversation like? Write a conversation based on what you see in the picture.

Conversations will vary. Encourage students to use the past tense in their

dialogues. You may wish to have students brainstorm verbs, nouns, and

adjectives they could use in their conversations.

_____

_____

_____

_____

_____

_____

🌀 ¡A DIVERTIRSE! 🌀   Nombre _____

¿Quién rompió la ventana?

Someone broke a window in the school yesterday. Sra. Estricta, the school principal, says that she heard the window break at 4:00 P.M. When she looked out the window, she didn't see anyone.

Look at the pictures and write what the suspects say they were doing. Then write the name of the person you think broke the window. (Note: *to break* is *romper,* a regular *-er* verb)

Julia: Yo colgué la ropa en mi ropero. _____

Hugo: Yo planché mi camisa (en mi casa). _____

Diego: Yo saqué fotos. _____

Carmen: Yo monté a caballo. _____

Delia: Yo jugué al tenis. _____

Ricardo: Yo me duché (en mi casa). _____

¿Quién rompió la ventana?   Delia rompió la ventana. _____

¿Cómo se dice?

Nombre _____

Textbook pages 254–258

A. Catalina is writing a letter to her friend Marta about her first trip to the ocean. Help her finish the letter by writing a word from the list in each blank.

una toalla	el salvavidas	✓ la playa	el protector solar
bronceada	tomé el sol	flotando	arena
barco de vela	acuático	quemado	una concha

You may wish to read the letter aloud quickly once before assigning students the exercise.

¡Hola, Marta!

¡Me encanta ir a ___**la playa**___! Estoy muy

___bronceada___ porque ayer ___tomé el sol___ toda la tarde.

Usé ___el protector solar___. Carlos no usó nada. Hoy le duele

mucho la espalda y está muy ___quemado___.

Cuando hace viento, me encanta pasear en ___barco de vela___.

También me encanta jugar con la ___arena___ y hacer

castillos. Hoy Carlos estuvo ___flotando___ sobre las olas. Yo

te voy a dar ___una concha___. Encontré una muy bonita en

la playa.

¡Nos vemos pronto!

Catalina

Enrichment: Have students write a paragraph about a trip to the beach. Encourage them to use the preterite tense when they can.

¿Cómo se dice?

Nombre _____

Textbook pages 259–263

○ **A.** This is what the Llorente family did yesterday at dinner time. Can you complete the sentences with the right names?

1. _____ **Alicia** _____ puso la mesa para la cena.

2. _____ **Carmen** _____ no pudo ponerse los zapatos porque le quedan pequeños.

3. _____ **Julio** _____ sirvió los platos para la cena.

4. _____ **Lucas** _____ se durmió frente al televisor.

5. _____ **Matías** _____ pidió las gafas a Elena.

Nombre _____

B. **What happened yesterday? Look at the pictures and write the missing verbs in the correct form.**

M Yo _____**pedí**_____ dos helados de chocolate.

1. Matilde tuvo mucho sueño y ____**se durmió**____ muy temprano.

2. Roberto y Pablo no ____**pudieron**____ ir al cine porque llegaron tarde.

3. Tú y yo ____**nos pusimos**____ vestidos rojos ayer.

C. **What can you see in these pictures? For each, write a sentence in the past to describe it.**

M **Las niñas se durmieron a las nueve.**

1. El niño pidió pollo.

2. El camarero sirvió unos helados a los niños.

3. Los niños se pusieron las botas y los abrigos.

¿Cómo se dice?

Nombre _____

Textbook pages 264–267

○ **A.** You had a great day at the beach. Now you're showing friends the pictures you took that day. Write *este, ese, aquel, esta, esa,* or *aquella* to complete each sentence describing the picture.

M

_____**Esta**_____ chica se llama Iris.

3.

_____**Este**_____ barco de vela está cerca.

6.

_____**Esa**_____ lancha es moderna.

1.

_____**Ese**_____ chico se llama Raúl.

4.

_____**Aquella**_____ chica está muy lejos.

7.

_____**Esta**_____ concha es bonita.

2.

_____**Esta**_____ sombrilla es de mi amiga.

5.

_____**Esa**_____ chica está flotando.

8.

_____**Aquel**_____ chico se llama Víctor.

Nombre _____

B. You are showing your friends the gifts you bought yesterday. You have them sorted into piles, some near and some far away. Complete each sentence using *estos, esos, aquellos, estas, esas* or *aquellas.*

M Compré todos _____**estos**_____ regalos. (Están muy cerca.)

Compré _____**aquellos**_____ anteojos. (Están muy lejos.)

1. Compré _____**estas**_____ camisetas para Adán. (Están muy cerca.)

2. Compré _____**esos**_____ libros de México. (No están muy cerca.)

3. Compré _____**aquellas**_____ novelas para mamá. (Están muy lejos.)

4. Compré _____**aquellos**_____ zapatos azules. (Están muy lejos.)

5. Compré _____**esas**_____ bolsas para mis tías. (No están muy cerca.)

6. Compré _____**estos**_____ discos nuevos. (Están muy cerca.)

C. Your friend Inés likes to talk about things that are far away, even when they really aren't! Complete each conversation.

M INÉS: ¡Mira la lancha!

RUDY: ¿_____**Esta**_____ lancha que está muy cerca de nosotros?

INÉS: No, _____**aquella**_____ lancha que está muy lejos.

1. SARA: ¡Mira los caracoles!

INÉS: ¿_____**Aquellos**_____ caracoles que están lejos?

SARA: No, _____**esos**_____ caracoles que están más cerca.

2. HUGO: ¡Mira las olas!

INÉS: ¿_____**Aquellas**_____ olas que están muy lejos?

HUGO: No, _____**esas**_____ olas que están más cerca.

¿Cómo se dice?

Nombre _____

Textbook pages 268–271

A. You are being interviewed for the school newspaper because you've become famous for your artwork. Answer each of the school reporter's questions by using the following expressions:

este fin de semana	✓ mi papá	mi maestro de estudios sociales
mis amigos y mi familia	escribir	
las personas que quieren nadar	el sábado	ponerlo en la playa
		hacer carteles

M ¿Para quién pintaste el cuadro de una lancha?

Lo pinté _____ **para mi papá.** _____

1. ¿Para qué son esos papeles blancos grandes?

Sirven _____ para hacer carteles. _____

2. ¿Para cuándo tienes que completar aquel cartel?

Tengo que completarlo _____ para el sábado. _____

3. ¿Para quiénes pintas tus cuadros y carteles?

Los pinto _____ para mis amigos y mi familia. _____

4. ¿Para qué sirven aquellos lápices?

Los lápices sirven _____ para escribir. _____

5. ¿Para qué escribiste ¡PELIGRO! en este cartel?

Lo escribí _____ para ayudar a la gente. _____

6. ¿Para quién es el cartel?

Es _____ para las personas que nadan. _____

7. ¿Para cuándo necesitas el cartel?

Necesito el cartel _____ para este fin de semana. _____

¡A leer!

Nombre _____

Read the following text. Then choose the best answer for the questions.

Los tiburones

Es tan común encontrar tiburones en el mar como pájaros en el cielo. Los tiburones viven en todo tipo de aguas: desde las aguas tropicales más calientes hasta las más frías, a muchas millas de profundidad. El tiburón de Groenlandia vive debajo de las enormes capas de hielo del Ártico.

Yo trabajé de buzo en un acuario de California unos años y pasé 11,000 horas debajo del agua, muchas veces acompañado de tiburones. No me dan miedo. Me gustan.

Quiero ir a bucear al mar Caribe, donde todavía hay muchos. Los tiburones son animales muy interesantes y me gusta estudiarlos debajo del agua.

Nota:
Tiburón means "shark."
Profundidad means "depth."
Hielo means "ice."

---

1. Los tiburones viven en _____.

   a. aguas frías

   b. aguas calientes

   c. aguas frías y calientes

2. ¿Dónde trabajó el autor del texto?

   a. Trabajó en un acuario.

   b. Trabajó en el mar.

   c. Trabajó en un barco.

3. ¿En dónde pasó el autor 11,000 horas?

   a. En el mar Caribe.

   b. En el acuario.

   c. Debajo del agua.

4. ¿Qué quiere hacer el autor en el mar Caribe?

   a. Quiere nadar.

   b. Quiere bucear.

   c. Quiere tomar el sol.

Nombre _____

Conexión con las matemáticas

Choose different items in your classroom that all students have different amounts of. Use this chart to find the average number that students have. Then write sentences about your results and compare them with a partner. Make sure to write out the numbers in words.

Cosa	Total de cosas		Total de alumnos	Promedio
lápices		÷		
libros				

1. El promedio de lápices en la clase es del _____ Answers will vary. ____.

2. El promedio de libros en la clase es del _____.

3. El promedio de _____ en la clase es del _____.

4. El promedio de _____ en la clase es del _____.

5. El promedio de _____ en la clase es del _____.

⚞ ¡APRENDE MÁS! ⚟

Nombre _____

You have learned to recognize cognates and to guess the meanings of words from context. Now it is time to practice. Read the following article from a book titled *¡Empecemos a charlar!* Underline the words you can guess because they are cognates, and circle the words you can guess from context. Finally, make a check mark above the words you look up in a Spanish-English dictionary. When you finish reading, count the number of words in each group. You may be surprised to find that you do not have to look up very many words! Instruct students to skim the article first, keeping their pencils on their desks. Briefly discuss what the article is about. Next, have students read the article more carefully, with pencils in hand.

El buceo

Puerto Rico es un lugar ideal para practicar los deportes acuáticos. Como está entre el

Atlántico y el Caribe, Puerto Rico tiene muchísimas playas... y dos mares por donde

se puede pescar y navegar. Además, las aguas cristalinas del Caribe son ideales

para el buceo. Puedes observar así una gran variedad de vida submarina y, si llevas

tu máquina especial, puedes sacar fotos interesantísimas del coral y de los

peces multicolores.

Los puertorriqueños y los miles de turistas que visitan la isla pueden disfrutar de

largos paseos por las playas, el esquí acuático, la pesca, la navegación en barco y el

buceo. Como el clima de Puerto Rico es tropical—la temperatura media es de 75°F

(24°C)—se pueden practicar estos deportes todo el año. Se practican además muchos

otros deportes en el país. El golf y el tenis son muy populares, así como el béisbol. Hay

muchos sitios donde puedes montar a caballo, ¡incluso puedes montar por la playa!

Extension: Write the three categories on the chalkboard: Cognates, Context, and Dictionary. Have students call out words from the article that go under each category.

¡A DIVERTIRSE!

Nombre _____

Busca las palabras

Read each sentence. Look in the puzzle for the words in heavy black letters. Each word may appear across, down, or diagonally in the puzzle. When you find a word, circle it. One has been done for you. The letters that are not circled form two secret words. Write the words in the sentence below the puzzle.

1. ✓ **Aquel** letrero dice ¡Se **prohíbe** nadar!

2. Pongo mi toalla sobre la **arena para tomar** el **sol.**

3. A veces hay **peligro** si vas a **bucear** en el mar.

4. **Esa** chica **quemada** navega en el **barco** de **vela.**

5. Primero **salí** del agua, y luego **comí** un helado.

6. ¿Te gusta el **esquí** acuático?

```
Q   P   R   O   H   Í   B   E   A   P
U   S   E   E   S   Q   U   Í   Q   U
E   A   O   L   A   E   C   R   U   P
M   L   T   L   I   O   E   R   E   A
A   Í   E   S   A   G   A   I   L   R
D   V   T   O   M   A   R   E   N   A
A   C   O   B   A   R   C   O   M   Í
```

A muchos turistas les encanta _____ **Puerto Rico** _____.

Nombre _____

A. You're going to the park and your mother wants to make sure that you know the way. Complete the directions she gives you with the correct word in parentheses.

M Voy a caminar una cuadra hacia el _____**este**_____ (derecha / este).

1. Luego voy a _____doblar_____ (doblar / este) a la derecha y caminar tres cuadras.

2. En la _____esquina_____ (cuadra / esquina) voy a doblar a la izquierda.

3. Voy a caminar dos _____cuadras_____ (derechas / cuadras) hacia el oeste.

4. Cerca del _____farol_____ (farol / oeste) está la entrada del parque.

Now draw a map showing the directions that your mother gave you above.

Nombre _____

B. You're in charge of watching your younger sister today. She just got home from playing soccer, and she's a mess! Tell her what she has to do according to her description.

M Tiene los zapatos sucios.

Quítate los zapatos. _____

1. Tiene la cara sucia.

Lávate la cara. _____

2. Tiene el pelo despeinado *(unkempt)*.

Péinate. _____

3. Tiene la ropa sucia.

Lava la ropa. _____

4. Tiene que estudiar para la clase de español.

Estudia para la clase de español. _____

5. Tiene sueño.

Acuéstate. _____

Nombre _____

C. Paula kept a diary this week, but she did not complete her entries. Help her complete the sentences in the past.

Ⓜ La semana pasada _____**fue**_____ (ser) muy larga.

1. El lunes _____**llegué**_____ (llegar) muy tarde a casa.

2. El martes Elsa y yo _____**jugamos**_____ (jugar) un partido de tenis.

3. El miércoles _____**fui**_____ (ir) al parque y _____**jugué**_____ (jugar) a fútbol.

4. El viernes _____**saqué**_____ (sacar) la basura y _____**sequé**_____ (secar) la ropa.

5. El sábado mamá y yo _____**compramos**_____ (comprar) mucha comida.

6. El domingo _____**hice**_____ (hacer) los deberes.

D. Now it's your turn to write about what you did last week. Use the verbs in the box.

ir	ser	hacer	abrir	jugar
estudiar	comer	estar	tener	

Ⓜ El lunes _____**llegué muy temprano a la escuela.**_____

1. El martes _____**Answers will vary.**_____

2. El miércoles _____

3. El viernes _____

4. El sábado _____

5. El domingo _____

Nombre _____

E. Write sentences that make sense by using phrases from each column. Use verbs in the past.

el miércoles	estar	frío
ayer	hacer	en la playa
esta mañana	tener	calor
durante las vacaciones		prisa

1. Answers will vary. _____

2. _____

3. _____

4. _____

5. _____

6. _____

Nombre _____

F. Write the word in each group that is not related to the other three.

M esquina, farol, cuadra, salvavidas _____ **salvavidas** _____

1. anillo, aretes, collar, calor _____ **calor** _____

2. caro, joyas, regalo, manzana _____ **manzana** _____

3. cuadra, playa, toalla, arena _____ **cuadra** _____

4. bronceado, cansado, quemado, protector solar _____ **cansado** _____

G. Gina wrote this postcard, but she forgot how to talk about the past! Use these verbs to complete her postcard about her day at the beach.

estar   poner   dormirse   pedir   poder   tener   servir

¡Hola Alicia!

Puerto Rico es muy bonito. Ayer Carlos y yo _____ **estuvimos** _____ en

la playa todo el día. Carlos no se _____ **puso** _____ crema

protectora y _____ **se durmió** _____ al sol. ¡Ahora está rojo como un

tomate! Ayer _____ **pedimos** _____ pescado fresco de cena, ¡qué rico!

Los camareros también nos _____ **sirvieron** _____ helado de frutas. La

semana pasada nosotros no _____ **pudimos** _____ bucear porque no

_____ **tuvimos** _____ tiempo, pero hoy vamos a hacerlo.

Un abrazo,

Gina

Nombre _____

H. You're with a friend on vacation at the beach. You see different things at a store in town. Draw two different versions of the items mentioned according to the descriptions. Then complete the descriptions, using the correct forms of *este, ese,* and *aquel.*

M _____Esta_____ sombrilla es grande.

_____Esa_____ sombrilla es más pequeña.

1. _____ traje de baño es muy bonito.

Pero _____ traje de baño es el más

bonito de la tienda.

2. _____ protector solar es caro.

_____ protector solar es barato.

3. _____ pantalones cortos son azules.

_____ son amarillos.

4. _____ toallas son de Maricel.

_____ toallas son de Mario.